CIVILITY RULES!

SHELBY JOY SCARBROUGH

CIVILITY
RULES
RULES!

CREATING A PURPOSEFUL PRACTICE OF CIVILITY

GEORGE WASHINGTON'S RULES REDEFINED

Forbes | Books

Copyright © 2020 by Shelby Joy Scarbrough.

All rights reserved. No part of this book may be used or reproduced in any manner whatsoever without prior written consent of the author, except as provided by the United States of America copyright law.

Published by ForbesBooks, Charleston, South Carolina.
Member of Advantage Media Group.

ForbesBooks is a registered trademark, and the ForbesBooks colophon is a trademark of Forbes Media, LLC.

Printed in the United States of America.

10 9 8 7 6 5 4 3 2 1

ISBN: 978-1-95086-340-2 (Hardcover)
ISBN: 979-8-88750-875-7 (Paperback)
ISBN: 979-8-88750-878-8 (eBook)
LCCN: 2020917422

Edited by Elayne Wells Harmer.
Cover design by Justin Bowens and Alex Ludovico of Clirror.
Layout design by David Taylor.

This custom publication is intended to provide accurate information and the opinions of the author in regard to the subject matter covered. It is sold with the understanding that the publisher, Advantage|ForbesBooks, is not engaged in rendering legal, financial, or professional services of any kind. If legal advice or other expert assistance is required, the reader is advised to seek the services of a competent professional.

Advantage Media Group is proud to be a part of the Tree Neutral® program. Tree Neutral offsets the number of trees consumed in the production and printing of this book by taking proactive steps such as planting trees in direct proportion to the number of trees used to print books. To learn more about Tree Neutral, please visit www.treeneutral.com.

Since 1917, Forbes has remained steadfast in its mission to serve as the defining voice of entrepreneurial capitalism. ForbesBooks, launched in 2016 through a partnership with Advantage Media Group, furthers that aim by helping business and thought leaders bring their stories, passion, and knowledge to the forefront in custom books. Opinions expressed by ForbesBooks authors are their own. To be considered for publication, please visit www.forbesbooks.com.

*To my mother and father, Pattie & Bill Scarbrough,
for always believing in me.*

CONTENTS

INTRODUCTION 1

CHAPTER ONE 7
George Washington, Can You Help Us?

CHAPTER TWO 15
The Power of Civility

CHAPTER THREE 23
Personal Responsibility

CHAPTER FOUR 29
Courtesy

CHAPTER FIVE 43
Humility

CHAPTER SIX 63
Empathy

CHAPTER SEVEN 83
Trust

CHAPTER EIGHT 103
Respect and Honor

CHAPTER NINE 115
My Practice of Civility

CONCLUSION. 119

WASHINGTON'S RULES OF CIVILITY &
DECENT BEHAVIOR IN COMPANY AND
CONVERSATION. 127

VARIATIONS ON THE GOLDEN RULE 141

ABOUT THE AUTHOR. 145

ACKNOWLEDGEMENTS. 149

ENDNOTES 155

The World We Make

by Alfred Grant Walton

We make the world in which we live
By what we gather and what we give,
By our daily deeds and the things we say,
By what we keep or we cast away.

We make our world by the beauty we see
In a skylark's song or a lilac tree,
In a butterfly's wing, in the pale moon's rise,
And the wonder that lingers in midnight skies.

We make our world by the life we lead,
By the friends we have, by the books we read,
By the pity we show in the hour of care,
By the loads we lift and the love we share.

We make our world by the goals we pursue,
By the heights we seek and the higher view,
By hopes and dreams that reach the sun
And a will to fight till the heights are won.

What is the place in which we dwell,
A hut or a palace, a heaven or hell
We gather and scatter, we take, and we give,
We make our world—and there we live.

INTRODUCTION

I can be an uncivil person.

At one time or another, we all are. Why? Because we're human. We all wrestle with pride and ego. The best part of understanding that right up front is that we already have something in common, and it is a good place to start.

One of the first steps to living civilly is discovering our common humanity. That means showing *real* compassion, understanding, humility, and forgiveness. Knowing that none of us is perfect is a good start; we all have room for improvement. Recognizing fallibility in ourselves, instead of complaining about it in others, inches us even closer to true civility.

This book is the result of my own development of what I call my "practice of civility." I make small improvements in my practice with each passing day, but I definitely and regularly fail. For example, I get upset when I see injustices happening to others; rude and inconsiderate behavior just pushes my buttons, and try as I might to bite my tongue, sometimes I just blurt out an unhelpful retort. I have yet to master the ability to be civil at all times, in all circumstances. When

I am the cause of or pulled into an uncivil interaction, I find myself disappointed in my behavior. I'm guessing we might also have that in common.

Maybe you hoped this book would reveal how to get *others* to be more civil. The uncomfortable truth is that we often focus only on *others'* thoughtless choices, *their* hypocrisy and selfishness, and *everyone else's* outright meanness. We give in to the temptation to point fingers at *them*. Maybe no one will look our way. God forbid anyone else find out we're not always being our best selves either!

But if we're going to get anywhere on this journey to civility, we must first acknowledge that each of our journeys starts with the word *I*. As in, *I* can be kinder. *I* can be more patient, more understanding, less demanding or judgmental. *I* can set an example of living a civil life with the humility required to live by example, without imposing it on others.

As part of this journey, I traveled to the Hoover Institution at Stanford University in California to interview my former boss, former Secretary of State George P. Shultz, about civility. When I asked him where we start to solve the challenges we face, he said, "It starts with *us*." We need to take ownership of our own roles in the quest for a more civil society.

The day we start taking personal responsibility for our own lives, we're ready to become positive contributors to society. The day we stop blaming others for the turbulent state of our world, we're one step farther along on the road to true peace in our hearts. We're that much closer to harmonious living with our fellow humans. If we are willing to look into our own hearts and work to adjust our own perspectives, we can embark on a journey to leading a more civil life. But I consider it a practice, like medicine and law: we must continually work on our civility if we are to master it. Although we will never be perfect, humans can become exceptional at civility with determination, effort, and practice.

In deciding to write this book, I embarked on a mission to persistently improve my own civility practice and—hopefully—to help anyone who wants to come with me on this journey to believe that we can restore civility to our homes, neighborhoods, workplaces, regions, and countries and even to our world.

But first things first. My immediate goal is to share how we can build a practice of civility in our own lives. With practice, patience, and prioritization, we can make positive change, one interaction at a time.

In addition to civility, another great passion in my life is finding and bringing joy to the world. I have a theory about the relationship between the two. If we are more civil, we will find more of the joy in the life that is right in front of us. If we are more joyful, civil behavior comes to us more easily.

There is nothing noble in being superior to some other man. The true nobility is in being superior to your previous self.

—W. L. Sheldon

Truly joyful people better manage anger and stress, loneliness, and loss. Joyful people have the ability to better traverse the sometimes-overwhelming challenges of humanity. That is not to say that joyful people have their heads in the sand or the clouds about reality. When we find even the simple joy in the tiniest of things, we bring positive energy to the world. Joy lifts us up, helps to buoy us through tough times, and allows us to remain civil.

I know the prescription works—I'm living proof. I am a more joyful and civil person than I was even a couple of years ago, and I believe that is positively affecting the people in my world and my relationships with them.

In the chapters that follow, I explore the deeper facets of human connection and interaction that I believe can lead to a more civil existence when practiced. While I have been studying, speaking, and writing about civility for more than a decade, I've become increasingly amazed by the complexity of the subject. As Einstein once reportedly said, "The more I learn, the more I realize how much I don't know." Just when I think I have it figured out, some societal shift happens, and I have to reevaluate my premise all over again. After all, civility involves human beings and our relationships. How many books have been written on *that* subject? Probably thousands. Welcome to mine: *Civility Rules!*

CHAPTER ONE

George Washington, Can You Help Us?

Perhaps you picked up this book because you're tired of all the fighting and you want to know if there's any hope that things will improve. Hostility and incivility are exhausting us all and creeping into every aspect of our lives, threatening our relationships and sense of well-being. How long will this last? Is this just the new normal?

Ironically, even though we're becoming more "civilized" over the centuries in the sense that we're part of a sophisticated and modern structure of government and countries, states, cities, and towns, we're becoming less civil as it relates to our humanity. While we're more electronically connected than ever, many of us feel increasingly disconnected and disengaged emotionally from one another.

We can technically "exist"—that is, breathe—without any human interaction whatsoever, thanks to the internet. With Google,

Facebook, Twitter, and YouTube, we can make snarky remarks anonymously with seemingly little repercussion. We can work remotely, text, or email instead of call, or we can use the Zoom app instead of meeting face to face. With the rise of artificial intelligence, robots and other technological innovations are fast becoming substitutes for people in the workplace.

But what does all this mean for the health of our political, economic, educational, and social systems? In the workforce of the future, we will need people who know how to mediate conflict. Until robots are fully sentient, leaders who are positive and solution oriented, who can forge solid human bonds, and who can reinvigorate or reinvent traditional relationships will be in high demand.

My initial interest in developing a practice of civility grew from life-changing experiences I had as a member of President Ronald Reagan's advance team at the White House and later as one of his protocol officers at the U.S. Department of State. I was able to observe how the president's own practice of civility defused international situations fraught with tension. During that time, and later as the president of my own company, Practical Protocol, my clients were heads of state and foreign ministers from around the world. I witnessed how empathetic, straightforward, and transparent communication between leaders can have a positive, lasting impact.

After working for President Reagan, I frequently lectured on cross-cultural business and diplomacy for some business-school programs. From those experiences, I have come to believe that the art of gracefully managing relationships is an essential first step.

Civility, to me, should be an integral component of civil society in general and of democracy in particular, as it is a key to clear, respectful communication. "Civility" and "civil society" are not redundant terms—there's a great distinction. (More on that in chapter 2.) A civil society does not mean a "polite and nice society"—it means a culture in which individuals have freedom of choice and work together for the greater good within a variety of institutions and organizations. Civility and civil society do have the same goal—finding a way to work together and raise the quality of life for all—but the means to achieving it differ. The words have the same root, but they aren't synonyms; you can have one without the other. A tribal group deep in the Amazon, for example, may have a high civility quotient in their individual and community relationships, while people in a complex, technologically advanced culture may be uncivil and self-centered.

We must be able to have difficult conversations, but we don't need to be uncivil to get our points across clearly and effectively. Uniting people in positive, collaborative relationships across this world's vast and evolving landscape is a moral imperative. The health of humanity, our personal happiness, our livelihoods, and maybe even our lives may depend more than ever upon connecting ourselves cooperatively and civilly to solve problems.

> *Never depend upon institutions or government to solve any problem. All social movements are founded by, guided by, motivated and seen through by the passion of individuals.*
>
> —**Margaret Mead**

Human relationships and civility have always mattered. In fact, we could go on a sociological journey back to the beginning of recorded human history to show how cooperation and communication are hallmarks of humankind. For the purposes of this book, however, we will look back just a couple of hundred years to explore civility in our society.

George Washington's Rules of Civility

For many years, I lived in the area of northern Virginia that was originally part of George Washington's estate. His home, Mount Vernon, was just a few miles from mine along a meandering tree-lined road called the George Washington Memorial Parkway. My husband at the time, Ben Jarratt, spent his college years at Washington and Lee University, where his education imprinted on him the responsibility to live up to the ideals of our first president. Sprinkled about our American colonial-style home was the lore of George Washington. His *Rules of Civility & Decent Behavior in Company and Conversation* had a prominent place on our bookshelf.

As a young man of fourteen, George recorded in the back of a school notebook, in his own beautiful handwriting, a list of inviolable tenets that would guide him throughout his life. Today, Washington is often credited as the author of "the rules," but he actually took them from a French etiquette book written by a Jesuit priest in 1595. The book offered practical advice to young noblemen who were destined to fill positions in high society.

I wondered how George Washington's rules of civility might apply today. Some of the guidelines seem very arcane compared to the way we now live, and perhaps they don't even apply anymore. For example, most of us never have to worry about "hearth etiquette": "Spit not in the fire, nor stoop low before it, neither put your hands into the flames to warm them, nor set your feet upon the fire, especially if there be meat before it" (rule 9).*

Most of the maxims in the guide, however, are timeless reminders

---

* The rules in their entirety are listed on pages 135-147.

to always look out for the comfort of others: "Sleep not when others speak, sit not when others stand, speak not when you should hold your peace, walk not on when others stop" (rule 6). And then there's empathy: "Show not yourself glad at the misfortune of another, though he were your enemy" (rule 22); simple respect: "Whisper not in the company of others" (rule 77); and just good old table manners: "Being set at meat, scratch not, neither spit, cough, or blow your nose, except [when] there's a necessity for it" (rule 90) and "Talk not with meat in your mouth" (rule 107).

Historians may debate whether young George was merely practicing his cursive writing skills when he recorded "the rules," but they agree on this point: he took these rules about civility to heart, becoming the serious and courteous man the guidelines depicted. Historian A. Ward Burian notes in his book *George Washington's Legacy of Leadership* that our first president dressed impeccably and often wore that solemn expression demanded by those centuries-old French rules of civility.[1] A model of decorum, Washington exuded a sense of dignity, no matter the circumstance. Washington clearly learned early on that a successful life is fueled by thoughtful, empathetic acts that ensure the comfort and well-being of one's fellow man. Based on how he conducted himself throughout his life, it's clear that the rules of civility and decent behavior seemed to stick with him. I believe they are still a great place to start when embarking on a practice of civility.

The directives are much more than mere mechanical, polite responses to social scenarios; rather, they focus on our relationships and interactions with each other through such qualities as courtesy, humility, trust, honor, and respect. Just as in Washington's day, we can look to timeless concepts that celebrate the fundamental values of civility. They worked centuries ago, they work now, and they can sustain us in the future—if we put them into practice.

How often do we actually get the chance to be part of something bigger than ourselves, as Washington was? Every day. The U.S. Constitution proclaims that one of our "certain unalienable rights" is the pursuit of happiness that President Washington and the Founding Fathers called for. But living the best version of life involves even more than pursuing our own happiness, as those same Founding Fathers knew. While we are encouraged to follow our individual paths, the Constitution also unites Americans under laws meant to benefit all society.

Civility Rules! offers an opportunity to learn more about the history, substance, and context of civility through the lens of Washington's "Rules of Civility." I hope that by the time you finish reading, you'll understand how to use the civility tools most effectively, and that you will want to put them into practice with me.

This book's title is both a hat tip to our first president's primary schoolwork and an exclamatory proclamation—as in, civility *rocks!*—to stimulate energy around the positive potential we could unleash if we each personally commit to a practice of civility. Civility is *not* an old-fashioned, archaic concept—we just all need to do our part to bring it back into focus. If we value civility as an important part of living together on this big blue marble as we "pursue happiness," we might just find a way to move forward together and accomplish great things together.

CHAPTER TWO

The Power of Civility

Why does civility matter? And what is the impact of the absence of civility? Civil behavior helps us encourage others to join us on our journey of self-improvement. It engenders respect for others as well as self-respect, raises the vibration of the human spirit, and contributes to the betterment of mankind. In short, our civility endows each of us with the ability to effect positive change.

Now, let's address a common snag in our thinking that we need to adjust: the idea that the world's challenges with incivility are insurmountable and that we can't contribute to solving them for the following reasons / excuses:

- Because we have no influence on change makers, leaders, and politicians. We are virtually invisible. We think to ourselves, *How can I make a dent in the problem? I am just one person.*

- Because every day we're bombarded with messages of incivility—like passengers in a plane experiencing maximum turbulence—and it can be so draining that we have no energy left to take on this challenge. We think, *I have no control.*

- Because we're experiencing conflict within our own families. Parents with tantrummy toddlers, temperamental tweens, or rule-testing teens know this firsthand. Even adult siblings and parents fight. We think in despair, *How can I practice civility in the world when I can't even manage it in my own family?*

- Because we're too busy scraping along at work to give any of our precious free time to this effort. And besides, the boss or the colleagues or the clients aren't civil, so why should *we* try? *They aren't civil, so I'm justified . . . right?*

At first glance, the preceding reasons seem to be pretty valid excuses to justify putting up with uncivil behavior. I hear you and acknowledge the legitimacy of those statements, but I invite you to come along with me on this journey to newfound civility in society. I ask you to suspend disbelief for the time being and ponder what would happen if we flipped the script and made the statements above into positively framed, actionable concepts.

As Hindu priest and international speaker Dandapani says, "Where awareness goes, energy flows."[2] In other words, if we are conscious of incivility in ourselves, we can work on changing. What we want to see in the world, we must *be* in the world (respectful nod to Gandhi). *We* have the power to do that. Every step closer matters. *We* matter. *We* can make a difference, starting with just our little corner of the world! We can only change ourselves, but sometimes that's all we need to do to change everything.

More Than Manners

Most people would say civility is about being kind to each other and having decent manners. That's a good start, but it's far from a complete consideration. The word *civility* comes from the Latin *civilis,* meaning "relating to citizens"; civility is behavior befitting a neighbor or kindred human being. Originally a political concept, it signifies "the actions and dispositions necessary to the smooth functioning of a civil society."[3] In his dictionary, Samuel Johnson defined it as "freedom from barbarity; the state of being civilised."[4] A "civil war" is a war between citizens of the same country—not a "polite" war.

At lunch one day, I was talking to a waiter about civility. (Yes, I ask everyone about their views on civility!) He told me his nephew was reprimanded in school for asking this question: "What's so 'civil' about the Civil War?" *Reprimanded?* I thought he should have been given an A in the class right then and there. It's a most poignant, insightful comment on the oxymoron "civil war." To me, it was an "out of the mouths of babes" kind of comment, strikingly mature in its logic and innocent in its reasoning.

I believe that being civil is *not* about being refined, cultured, educated, or belonging to high society. Yes, the word "civility" sounds calm and dignified; some might even say it feels unapproachable. But don't mistake civility's sometimes formal connotation for stiffness or its solemnity for affectedness or elitism.

Civility is about so much more than paying lip service to good manners in order to win a promotion, a bonus, or a popularity contest. Genuine civility is not about using rehearsed charm to persuade other people to do our bidding. Real civility—which does, of course, incorporate good manners—is actually selflessness.

It's about recognizing the humanity in the people around us and in ourselves so we can find our way forward together in life, even if we disagree with each other.

Civility—unpretentious, generous-of-heart behavior—raises us all. It's a win-win when it's implemented.

The Interplay between Civility and Freedom

George Washington overcame powerful forces opposed to a free nation and led with courage, dignity, and hope in the founding of an ambitious experiment. He walked into his leadership with a thorough education on the rules of getting along, thanks in part to his scribing the guidebook on civil behavior. While he led the American colonies in a long and grueling war against the British, our first president never lost sight of the end goal: to restore order, civility, and peace and then to protect and unleash freedom.

You might wonder how the concept of freedom manifests itself with civility. I have concluded that the two intersect at the point of free speech. Incivility shuts down discourse, while real civility encourages open lines of communication and the freedom to share ideas among ourselves.

In a speech I attended on the campus of Freedoms Foundation at Valley Forge, Pennsylvania, former California Lieutenant Governor John Harmer said, "Without civility, there can be no true freedom." Harmer served with then-governor Reagan during a particularly uncivil time in California's history.

Lieutenant Governor Harmer's statement stuck with me because he helped me see civility as imperative for the continuation of democracy. One voice is not a democracy. If we are so culturally battered that only one voice can be heard, only one voice tolerated while all others are dismissed as racist or Communist or fascist or liberal or conservative or hateful or cynical, we're letting our democracy evaporate.

Freedom depends on civility. Societies in which no one criticizes the government aren't civil—they're thought prisons. The easy way out might seem to be enacting laws that dictate the ways we must be civil. But legislating civility is just another example of giving our freedoms away to governmental control. It's a George Orwell, *1984* sort of world. I believe all thoughtful adults are capable of protecting themselves in conversation with others—we don't need to give Big Brother the right to determine how we engage with others and how we exchange ideas. This is on *us*. This is up to *us*.

Civility is not about what we must *refrain* from saying to avoid hurting another's feelings. It's about saying exactly how we feel and what we believe in a way that will be heard and understood—gently enough so that we will be motivated to think through our own beliefs and ponder change.

Of course, I want to acknowledge the importance of defending "what is right." But how can we do that without increasing division? It's not easy. How can we be civil yet stand up to truly unacceptable behavior, such as racism and bigotry? On our path toward more civility, how do we balance the fight against injustice with our desire to resist conflict? How can civility and righteousness coexist when we all have different opinions? Who is actually right? Now *that's* easy—I am! Wait. Maybe that other guy has a point.

We need to remember that human beings have different backgrounds, traditions, values, financial situations, and so on. We don't have the same opportunities or experiences. Sadly, we just don't see everything through the same lens. For example, not everyone believes in God and divine intervention. Some people never vote, while others are passionate about civic responsibilities.

We must extend to others the freedom to be different from ourselves without judging. Judgment is not within our purview; it's not our job.

Some actually encourage division, because their perception of justice doesn't fit with a narrative of being civil, and they want to do it their way—the "correct" way. They are convinced they are on the righteous path, and there is no place for civility when others are wrong or evil or . . .

I believe it's crucial that we renew a commitment to civility as a tool for securing the future of freedom. Let's build bridges of communication and learn how to tolerate and understand ideas other than our own. Let's learn to discuss and dissent while expanding our belief in the freedom of expression.

President Reagan said, "Freedom is never more than one generation away from extinction. It has to be fought for and defended by each generation."[5] Americans have fought long and hard for freedom of speech. We can't let it slip away merely because we're not sure how to behave civilly—or how to demonstrate civility when we encounter its opposite.

Five Tenets of Civility for a Modern Audience

I soaked up George Washington's guide with admiration for his dedication to the practice of the art of civility. It seems to me that the greatest among us are often the humblest and most earnest, just like our first president. He wasn't afraid to tackle both lofty ideals and simple acts. Everything he did, including eventually releasing the slaves he inherited as a child, was not for personal glory but for the greater good. One might say that even his practice of civility was a lifelong pursuit—it wasn't until right before he died that Washington decreed the freeing of generations of slaves that were part of his estate. He was a student of civil behavior in an ever-changing world until the day he left it.

In my ponderings on Washington's *Rules of Civility & Decent Behavior in Company and Conversation*, I was looking for the "why" behind the "what"—how the rules are contextual for our time.

This is what I found: the concept of civility itself can be broken down to the five core ideals of courtesy, humility, empathy, trust, and honor/respect. These principles are the subjects of separate chapters within *Civility Rules!*

Each chapter contains principles that illuminate the meaning of these societal standards, incorporating insights, anecdotes, and experiences from everyday people like you and me. I also researched the views of thought leaders throughout history and interviewed similar modern-day leaders to build a small collection of quotes on civility. I'll share some tools and offer a methodology I use to deflect or soften uncivil behavior. I hope this is where we might all find common ground.

We must all learn how to coexist productively and peaceably on this planet, while, at the same time, celebrating the freedom of the individual to be a unique and independent being. That's all. That's how we build a civil society. And it's a DIY solution—it doesn't cost anything or take much time or require influence. The *lack* of civility, on the other hand, could cost us everything. Even when we're tired or distracted or triggered when confronted with uncivil behavior, we can still incorporate a practice of civility into our lives. We'll explore all of this in the following pages of *Civility Rules!*

CHAPTER THREE

Personal Responsibility

Labor to keep alive in your breast that little spark of celestial fire called conscience.

—*Rule 110*

The concept of personal responsibility is the thread that silently weaves through the virtues, values, and character traits explored in the coming pages. Jim Rohn, an American entrepreneur and motivational speaker, said, "You cannot change the seasons, but you can change yourself."[6] He reminds us to come to terms with what we can control and what we cannot. My friend Diane Brown uses a phrase in her teaching: "Control the controllables." So much of life is out of our control. The one thing we have influence over is how we behave and being accountable for that behavior.

When I was fifteen years old, my parents started what would become a forty-year journey as owners of Burger King restaurants.

My sisters and I worked in every position: cashier, cook, cleaner, you name it. No excuses, no slacking, no special preferences. Regular employees. During this time, they started to teach us to "think like an owner." It did not mean we could walk around with an attitude like we owned the place; rather, it meant constantly looking around for a way to improve the restaurant, help another crew member, clean up our messes, show initiative, and take responsibility if we made a mistake and learn from it.

To me, being personally responsible means owning my own life, taking charge of the course of life and not leaving it up to anyone or anything. Things happen, sure, but how we respond to them is up to us. Doing so takes courage, acceptance of our imperfections, and a realistic view of life.

The demise of personal responsibility occurs when we resort to blaming people or circumstance for something within our control. Personal responsibility is not an innate ability in all people, but we are capable of learning the skills required. We can practice a few habits that make us more accountable:

1. Keep our commitments with other people. If we must back out, let the other party know the reason, without excuses.

2. Respect other people's time.

3. Train ourselves to not take anything personally.

4. Catch ourselves when we start to blame others.

5. Refuse to complain.

6. Find something joyful to focus on, and express gratitude.

7. Work on self-love.

8. Apologize and own our mistakes, and then work to grow and learn from those mistakes.

By no means is admitting to ourselves that we make mistakes or are imperfect an easy pill to swallow. However, when we become aware of the proven effects of being accountable for our actions, the long-term gain from our accountability to ourselves far outweighs the short-term discomfort of admitting we were wrong or cleaning up a mistake.

As a protocol officer at the U.S. Department of State under Ambassador Lucky Roosevelt, one of my favorite times was when the team gathered to debrief after a "visit."* My immediate supervisors were two people I would come to cherish: Deputy Chief of Protocol Catherine "Bunny" Murdock and Assistant Chief of Protocol Julie Andrews Petersmeyer. Bunny loves a good drama but hates sloppy protocol. Her management style was to ask us, "What's the story?" That was our cue to recount all the things that had gone wrong on the visit, and we would laugh and grimace and have a moment of shared humanity.

Bunny would subtly coach us by asking, "So, what could we have done differently?" She knew that no visit would ever be perfect and there were always going to be stories to tell. However, this was our time to own our errors and our opportunity to take responsibility and continually hone our craft. I am eternally grateful for that training.

Looking back on those days in the offices of Presidential Advance and Protocol, the best reminiscing and stories come from the disasters (or almost-disasters) and mistakes. We try to get together once a year,

---

* The Protocol Office hosts the visits of heads of state, presidents, kings, queens, and prime ministers. I was a "visits" officer who coordinated all the logistics of those visits, as opposed to a "ceremonials" officer who focused on luncheons, dinners, and ceremonies.

and in an environment of trust and respect, we share hilarious, sad, anxiety-ridden, and all-around amazing stories of the mishaps with world leaders. Shhhh. I'll never tell.

As I began my journey of putting all my thoughts down on paper, I had a long talk with my friend Andrew Sherman, partner at Seyfarth Shaw law firm in Washington, D.C., longtime outside counsel for the Entrepreneurs' Organization, and author of more than thirty business books. Needless to say, he thinks a lot and doesn't sleep much.

He shared with me the following insights:

> James Redfield wrote a great book called *The Celestine Prophecy*, and it's guided my entire life and career in many, many ways. In the book he teaches that everyone, every single person you meet, has a message for you, has a lesson for you. If you approach life as if everyone you meet and everyone you work with and everyone in their supply chain and everyone in the distribution channel has something to teach you, number one, it humbles you. You can get excited about interacting with other people. You get excited about meeting people with backgrounds different than your own. It's not somebody that you would be discriminatory toward if it's somebody you welcome. Every day I try and learn something. Every day I try and teach something.
>
> Something that gravely concerns me is we are at an age of probably the most extreme levels of divisiveness that we've ever had. If we start demonizing "others," we're creating a whole other level of economic divisiveness and educational divisiveness and technology divisiveness. That alone is a case for increased civility efforts.
>
> So, then there's the business case for civility. There's the sort of socio-political case. There's the moral and ethical case. And then there's the legal consequences; the more that bubbles up in our society that holds people

accountable for everything that they do, is sort of the scarier part of civility. What advances us as mankind is the civility that's rooted in our chosen behaviors, not in the behaviors where HR or some courthouse or law firm beats us into submission. True civility needs to be a "want to," not a "have to." You know the difference between authentic civility and me pretending to be nice to you because HR told me to or because I risk a lawsuit or because I don't want you writing something nasty about me on Facebook. We should be civil to each other because we *want* to be, not because we *have* to be.[7]

What would our lives look like when we are fully responsible for our actions? According to Linda Galindo, author of *The 85% Solution: How Personal Accountability Guarantees Success, No Nonsense, No Excuses*, we experience decreased stress, we up our productivity and improve our relationships, and we love and respect ourselves more.

Why is personal responsibility important for the practice of civility? Accountability builds trust with the important people in our lives. People who blame others for the ills of their own lives cause others to turn around and run away. It becomes difficult to build lasting relationships built on trust and respect when your friend or colleague is chronically late, does not own up to mistakes, or finds fault in others but never seems to see their own failings. It's just a bummer.

CHAPTER FOUR

Courtesy

Read no letters, books, or papers in company, but when there is a necessity for the doing of it, you must ask leave.

—*Rule 18*

Be not forward but friendly and courteous, the first to salute, hear, and answer, and be not pensive when it's a time to converse.

—*Rule 66*

Gaze not on the marks or blemishes of others and ask not how they came.

—*Rule 71*

Rinse not your mouth in the presence of others.

—*Rule 101*

Woven throughout Washington's rules is an emphasis on the importance of courtesy. I see courtesy as the highway or the network on which the values of civility move. For example, the courtesy of not interrupting someone conveys the value of respect. Offering someone the food on the table before you take any is about honoring the other person. Telling the truth is about trust . . . and so on.

Now, let's tease out the difference between these three terms: *civility, courtesy,* and *manners*. Do they mean the same thing? Most of us would lump them all together—in fact, most dictionaries list them as synonyms—but each word carries its own important and distinct meaning.

We looked at a couple of definitions of civility in the introduction, but here's one more: The *Oxford English Dictionary* (OED) defines *civility* as "conformity to the principles of social order, behavior befitting a citizen; good citizenship."[8]

The OED defines *courtesy* as "considerateness in intercourse with others" and "nobleness, generosity, benevolence, goodness."[9]

And the OED defines *manners* as "external behavior in social intercourse, estimated as good or bad according to its degree of politeness or of conformity to the accepted standard of propriety" and "habits indicative of good breeding."[10] Among the three words we're examining, only *courtesy* includes "politeness" in its definition. Even so, courtesy is much, much more than simply being polite.

I find it useful to think of *civility* as the end goal and the most all-encompassing of the three words. It's timeless; universal truths of social order and goodness are always relevant. It embraces all the ideals of humility, empathy, trust, honor, and respect.

When I think of courtesy, I picture it as a bridge that carries us to civility. Courtesy is the social contract we enter into just by virtue of being human. It's the expectation to embrace the Golden Rule:

to treat others as we would wish to be treated. Courtesy is civility in action, made real in the world when we make daily choices based on our commitment to being civil.

OK, so where do manners fit in to this picture?

Well, manners are a subset of courtesy. They're the practical actions we take to demonstrate courtesy to each other: opening doors, making eye contact, nodding and smiling to acknowledge someone's presence as we walk past them. Imagine courtesy as that sturdy bridge, and then imagine that our manners are the cars that travel on it.

The key to remember here is that just as car styles change over time, much of what society considers "manners" also changes over time. Although the principle of showing courtesy doesn't change, the transport mechanism (manners) adjusts as traditions and cultural norms change.

In a post-COVID-19 world, this point is even more relevant. For example, standing six feet away to speak to a friend in 2019 might have been perceived as standoffish and poor manners. In 2020, however, it's become an essential standard operating procedure during a pandemic and—at least for now—more courteous to our fellow humans. What constitutes "manners" will continue to change and evolve depending on the circumstances of the time.

Washington's Example of Courtesy

Courtesy played an important role not only in the founding of our country but also in the continued existence of our young nation. Historian Richard Brookhiser, author of *Founding Father: Rediscov-*

ering George Washington, noted that our first president considered courtesy to all as imperative to create an egalitarian society:

> All modern manners in the Western world were originally aristocratic. "Courtesy" meant behavior appropriate to a court. [. . .] Yet Washington was to dedicate himself to freeing America from a court's control. Could manners survive the operation? [. . .]
>
> Without realizing it, the Jesuits who wrote [the original rules of civility], and the young man who copied them, were outlining and absorbing a system of courtesy. [. . .] When the company for whom decent behavior was to be performed expanded to the nation, Washington was ready.[11]

Kevin Butterfield, executive director of the Fred W. Smith National Library for the Study of George Washington at Mount Vernon, offers another insight into our first president's commitment to courtesy: Washington recognized that in a nonhierarchical society like the United States, where people no longer had to defer to their "betters," good manners still had value. In a republic, where supreme power is held by the people, the people's behavior matters. In a republic, each citizen has a personal obligation and responsibility to build the nation's character by building their own.

Contrast that duty with the responsibility of citizens in a hierarchical society. People ruled by a dictator or czar don't have a political duty to be courteous to each other, as long as they are loyal to their leader. It doesn't matter how they behave toward one another—everything depends on their ruler.

To preserve a republic, however, its citizens have an obligation to be civil to each other. We can't abdicate our personal responsibility to our leaders—to do so is to invite dictators. We each must do our part. George Washington realized that courteous behavior is a vital lubricant that allows societies to function more smoothly. What was true then is still true today. The demonstration of courtesy is an easy way to build a bridge to empathy and understanding. It's simple: put others first.

Throughout Washington's entire life, people talked about his stellar character and how he carried himself in society. Butterfield states, "Washington had a sort of grace, a deportment, a way of presenting himself to the world that would have belonged in court, in the finest houses in Europe. He had an ability to carry himself with real dignity. But he did it in a really non-ostentatious way."[12]

Butterfield and Brookhiser remind us that Washington's grasp of civility helped save our nation more than once. His ability to maintain his cool in the face of bloody aggression during the war—and a flood of dangerous antagonism after the war—brought a resolve and stability that cemented this nation's foundations. We modern-day Americans can emulate our first president's commitment to this principle. Through civility, we can still be the torchbearers of freedom and democracy for all.

Washington knew that if we embrace the courtesies that lead us to a civil society, we can change the course of our national future, which affects the well-being of the whole world. We want to be able to speak openly and confidently with our neighbors about the importance of a civility movement. The goal is to open hearts to the idea that civility—as opposed to antagonism, hatred, and violence—is the long path to positive, lasting change.

Learning Appropriate Manners

Since manners are a means of crossing the bridge of courtesy on the road to civility, they are still an important part of achieving a sustainable practice of civility. While they may vary from one era to the next, or one culture to the next, some manners have been used by courteous people for centuries.

Take the act of shaking hands, for example. This tradition began in the Western world as a way to show that someone didn't have a gun in their hand—they came in peace. Whether it occurred on disputed territory a few centuries ago or in a boardroom today, the handshake has been a staple of civility—or at least it was, until the COVID-19 pandemic. Even though we may not shake hands again for some time, we can and must continue to find ways to show we come in peace. Our method of greeting can still acknowledge another human being with respect, whether it's bumping elbows, bowing slightly (as in Japanese culture), nodding our head, or pressing our hands together in front of our hearts (as is done in much of India).

> *Courtesy is as much a mark of a gentleman as courage.*
>
> —attributed to Theodore Roosevelt

Other good manners have lost their usefulness over the years—in part simply due to better hygiene. For example, take Washington's rule 13: "Kill no vermin as fleas, lice, ticks, etc., in the sight of others." And we don't really care today who puts their hat on first in a group of people (rule 27)! However, the point of that rule makes sense: an awareness of "who does what first" helps a host courteously convey cues so we know what to expect and how to act.

I don't read etiquette books. When I need an answer to such questions, I just call Rick Ahearn, my first boss on the 50th Presidential Inaugural Committee when I moved to Washington, D.C. He is a walking encyclopedia of proper behavior. He's so proper that he is subjected to constant ribbing from our advance office crew. But what a teacher he was to me!

What's considered good manners also varies according to culture. Because of that, it's an act of courtesy itself to learn about an unfamiliar culture and its customs prior to a visit. For example, burping after a meal is a no-no in American culture. But in many countries in Asia, it's a compliment to the cook for the host to belch *loudly* after a meal—conveying satisfaction. When we dig into the meaning behind certain etiquette practices around the world, we find that their origins all share the common aim: to be courteous.

Even in the United States, our definition of "good manners" varies from region to region, but pointing out a visitor's deficiency in locally practiced cultural niceties is itself discourteous. Instead, we can appreciate warm and generous behavior and intentions, which are the true hallmarks of good manners.

Manners are about making those around you feel comfortable and respected. The great satirist Jonathan Swift wrote this definition more than two centuries ago: "Good manners is the art of making those people easy with whom we converse. Whoever makes the fewest people uneasy is the best bred in the company."[13]

Whenever we're unsure about how to behave appropriately, we can't panic. Remember that good manners are ultimately about showing other people we appreciate and respect them.

My friend Cindy Boyd and I travel together a lot. We both enjoy journeys, and we have found that we are quite compatible traveling companions. It didn't take long before we would show up in a hotel room and just start rearranging it to our liking without talking about it. We don't ask who wants which bed or which sink, we just know. We both keep our worlds neat and tidy to respect the other's space, and we are sometimes courteous to a fault. At one dinner, I offered her the last drops of wine from the bottle. Quoting an idiom she learned in Guatemala, she replied, "No, *you* have the last drops of happiness." Wanting to be courteous, I said, "No, *you* please have the last drops of happiness," and so on until we were in a mock fight about it. "Fighting" about who is going to be more courteous than the other—that works for me. It wasn't a competition for who was nicer, it was and is a genuine desire to honor each other.

For the most part, the right intention—a heart that wants to sincerely connect and honor another person's dignity—will win the day, even if we miss the mark by using "incorrect" customs. Of course, we can always follow our host's lead or simply *ask*. I also find that a little humility comes in handy in many an awkward situation!

Must We *Always* Be Courteous?

Life is complicated, and we inevitably encounter ugliness in humanity. We face cruelty, opposition, lack of understanding, bias, and more. But in the midst of that, we still need to talk to each other.

Here's the starting point: Can we curb our irritated remarks to or about strangers, workmates, family, and friends when our patience is wearing thin? We may still *think* uncivil thoughts, because we're human. But a big part of civility (and adulthood) is filtering our spontaneous thoughts and controlling our actions.

For the next quiet Uber driver who ignores our friendly greeting, we'll let the person be, instead of giving a one-star rating. We might even gently ask how their day is going. Maybe, as I discovered one time, the driver is slightly deaf. Maybe the last passenger was rude, or maybe their cat died. Maybe they're worried about how to pay the bills. We never know what's going on in someone's life—*even those people we think we know well*. Even if our courteous behavior is unrequited, perhaps we can try even harder to give others the benefit of the doubt, to see the best in them.

Ralph Waldo Emerson wrote, "We must be as courteous to a man as we are to a picture, which we are willing to give the advantage of a good light."[14] Just as we hope that others will focus on our strengths and ignore our weaknesses, we can freely give others the same courtesy, with little cost to our own ego.

Communicating the Right Message

My hope is to offer scaffolding and tools that we can rely upon to better communicate with each other, a central theme of civility. Courteous, two-way communication is essential in problem-solving. Granted, all-out war is an option, but that is the least preferred method for a civilized society to fix its problems. However, we might think of incivility as a precursor to war—an early warning sign.

In 2020, with unrest in the United States due to disparate political perspectives, racial tensions, and the pandemic-caused economic upheaval, we are facing a significant choice. We are coming to a juncture in our history. Shall we dissolve into factions, camps, and total anarchy, or shall we rise to a more inclusive and compassionate level of civil society? Which road will we choose to take?

My work as a protocol officer at the State Department set conditions for positive diplomatic interactions and fruitful dialogue. Creating and promoting situations in which people can speak and actually be heard is something I love to do. It's personally and professionally fulfilling to participate in making our world more civil. Any protocol officer, communications professor, or foreign emissary will tell you that diplomacy reduces friction and keeps doors open so that ideas can be exchanged.

Dr. Scott Talan, a communications professor at American University in Washington, D.C., acknowledges that crafting a message so that people can truly hear it is quite challenging, considering the complexities of modern life. We're faced with an explosion of social media in many different directions: blogs, YouTube channels, podcasting, and more. New apps pop up every day, and the TikTok mobile video craze is perfectly tailored to those with micro-attention spans. Combine constantly fluctuating developments with ADHD and screen addiction, and you get a recipe for distractibility and overstimulation that makes it difficult for even the simplest message to break through.

Dr. Talan has a straightforward everyday example that explains how challenging communication can be. Take a happily married couple, for instance. One spouse says, "I love you" to the other spouse every day at 6:00 p.m. In theory, this should work, right? Marital bliss should ensue. The spouse is sending the message to the right receiver. Three little words.

However, what if those words are spoken in the same monotonous voice, at the same time every day. Where's the spontaneity? The joy? At some point, the receiving spouse may begin to doubt the sincerity of the sending spouse because their words sound robotic, planned, unspontaneous. In all likelihood, eventually the receiving spouse may begin to feel that there is no genuine feeling behind the words.

> *Courtesies of a small and trivial character are the ones which strike deepest in the grateful and appreciating heart.*
>
> —*attributed to Henry Clay*

To avoid communication glitches like this, Dr. Talan recommends that we think about who our audience is and whether the message is relevant to them in that time and place. In this case, our sender got both aspects of communication right. But we have to go a step further and examine the method of transmission. If you're the sender of the message, Dr. Talan suggests mixing up the means. In our example, Post-it notes, dinners, cards, chocolate, or kisses all say "I love you" without actually speaking the words and with a little element of surprise and novelty. Let's get our sender to bring a bouquet of heart-shaped balloons to the receiving spouse—but not every evening at six o'clock!

On the other hand (just to confuse the issue), small repetitive acts that show appreciation for and to another person can also be a magnificent way to communicate feelings. The key difference is that *both parties* must understand that the act is, in fact, an agreed-upon tradition or ritual that brings comfort and joy—a code, say, like a sign-off phrase on a phone call that both understand to be a signal expressing love, gratitude, or appreciation. Something that small can raise serotonin levels—what I call the "joy juices" in our brains—that can physiologically help us feel love and affection for another person.

And we're just talking about simple messages communicated between two people who know and trust each other. As we all know from our own experience, even a message with good intentions has the capacity to fall short of the mark. Think about a time when someone you loved and trusted misinterpreted a message from you that you thought was so clear. Now imagine what happens when the message is complex, between parties that may not know or trust each other. All kinds of things can go wrong in the transmission of that message. If both parties practice courtesy, positive communication and bonding can hopefully commence.

Dr. Talan has some wise words regarding the challenge of conveying the right message: Remember that in a crisis or sticking point in communication, if we have already worked hard to build up respect, trust, and good will along the way, we are more likely to be given the benefit of the doubt.

Dr. Richard Haass, president of the Council on Foreign Relations, has some experience in reacting civilly in a tense situation. The nonpartisan think tank he leads publishes *Foreign Affairs*, an internationally respected magazine that provides an in-depth analysis of U.S. foreign policy and diplomacy. Dr. Haass says civility can be demonstrated with tone, respect, and manners, not necessarily with words and treaties. We can disagree without being disagreeable.

"Just because you disagree doesn't necessarily make someone your enemy or your adversary," he says. "It's always useful to maintain a kind of ability to talk and work together, even if you don't agree at the moment. You don't want to preclude the ability to talk or agree at a later moment. Or you may simply ban the area of disagreement. If you are going to disagree over the substance, you don't need to add to it a whole extra layer of shouting or abuse. Why poison the relationship? Why kill off the ability to communicate?"[15]

If we're having a heated exchange of ideas, and the other party detours from the substance of the conversation in an inflammatory way, communication breaks down. So what can we do? Dr. Haass told me, "Sometimes people feel the pressure to be uncivil to get noticed. I always push back and say, 'Just be smart. Being smart is good enough. If you're smart on a regular basis, you'll get noticed.'"

If the conversation completely deteriorates, it's time to back off and establish some rules for engagement. Occasionally, people need to cool off first. If that's the case, come back later with those rules of engagement, and start again. Remember to be smart, as Dr. Haass recommends. Stay patient. Be courteous. And don't give up. If we want to deliver a message, we have to keep trying.

It pays to be courteous, since the price we pay for uncivil behavior can be quite high. If we're wise, we'll strive to earn goodwill points as we go, because obstacles in the road to good communication and getting along will inevitably appear. But can we still speak our minds, or do we have to bite our tongues to stay civil?

"This is a pretty intense world we live in," Dr. Haass says. "My view is you've got to comment. In no way does it mean you filter the content. In no way does it mean you even filter the intensity of your positions. It means you filter how you act on or express your positions. Societies work, in part, not just because we have rules, but because we have degrees of restraint. That's what it takes to have day-in, day-out relationships.

"For anyone who believes that civility, or simply the appearance of civility, counteracts substance, remember this," Dr. Haass continues. "You can be civil at the same time you're issuing a declaration of war.

"We need protocols, we need structure, in order to keep the channels of communication open," he explains. "Civility, to some extent, is about the ability to keep open a working relationship. It doesn't dilute or sandpaper off the content. It's simply about making communications possible."

The most important message I can send about the importance of civility is to remind people of this paradox: we can fight metaphorical wars and, in the strangest of ways, still get along. We can separate the substance of our disagreements—our valid opinions—from the means by which we deliver our messages. We can ensure that a courteous means of delivery keeps at least a crack of our opponent's door open.

CHAPTER FIVE

Humility

Strive not with your superiors in argument, but always submit your judgment to others with modesty.

—Rule 40

Undertake not to teach your equal in the art [he] himself professes; it flavors of arrogance.

—Rule 41

Play not the peacock, looking everywhere about you to see if you be well decked...

—Rule 54

A man ought not to value himself of his achievements or rare qualities of wit, much less of his riches, virtue, or kindred.

—Rule 63

Before we start this chapter, I have to admit that even putting pen to paper on this topic makes me a little uncomfortable. As I dove deeper and deeper into the subject, I realized how complex humility really is and how little I understood its value. Who am I to write about humility? Am *I* humble? Then I realized that even pondering that question means I am not truly humble. After pressing through the research, I came to believe that the core, primary anchor for civility is humility.

We might start to truly understand humility if we start with what humility is not. Humility is not a weakness. It's not servility or being a doormat or nonassertive.

Although the word *humble* is often used to describe someone who is self-deprecating, passive, or timid, the word's true meaning couldn't be more different. British theologian C. S. Lewis wrote:

> Do not imagine that if you meet a really humble man he will be what most people call 'humble' nowadays. [. . .] Probably all you will think about him is that he seemed a cheerful, intelligent chap who took a real interest in what you said to him. [. . .] He will not be thinking about humility: he will not be thinking about himself at all.[16]

American pastor Rick Warren said it more succinctly: Humility isn't "thinking less of ourselves," he said, "but thinking of ourselves *less*."[17]

Humility is also distinct from modesty. While many dictionaries list the two words as synonyms, when we look into their origins, we can see how much they differ.

Psychiatrist and philosopher Neel Burton explained that modesty means "restraint in appearance and behavior: the reluctance to flaunt oneself, to put oneself on display, or to attract attention."[18] Derived from the Latin word *modus* ("measure" or "manner"), modesty implies an outward behavior. "At best," Burton wrote, "modesty is no more than good manners," an external, outward-facing demeanor that's often merely skin deep. The phrase "false modesty" is used to describe a disingenuous or superficial person. False modesty leads us to trust that person a little less, so in a sense it's an aspect of uncivil behavior.

Humility, on the other hand, has to do with inner beauty. Its Latin root is from *humilis* ("lowly"), which in turn is from *humus* ("ground" or "earth"). This makes sense. Think of how we describe people who can subdue their ego as "down to earth." True humility, Burton believes, "derives from a proper perspective of our human condition: one among billions on a small planet among billions." The word *humility* implies a genuineness of spirit. People are drawn to those who continuously and genuinely exhibit such qualities—we instinctively trust them.

Someone who possesses authentic humility is likely thoughtful, considerate, understanding, and compassionate—in short, someone who values and respects others.

Even after looking at root words and parsing definitions, though, the concept of humility is still a little elusive to me. It's easier to say, "I know it when I see it." Trying to develop humility within a practice of civility is even trickier, because just when we decide we've achieved it, by definition, we're no longer humble. Innately humble people don't think about how humble they are. This conundrum is why it's taken me so long to write this chapter! Is humility something we are born with, or can we develop it? If we develop it, is it authentic or contrived?

The Templeton Foundation is an organization that awards grants for studies on "intellectual humility." It's pretty fascinating to look over all the research. I honestly don't know what half the titles even mean! The studies are very academic—a lot of data and reports validate the findings. To me, it's pretty basic: those who exhibit intellectual humility simply recognize they are fallible and are open to learning about anything. We are at our most civil when we show respect for other philosophies while pursuing an honorable life based on our own earnest beliefs.

THE SERVANT-LEADER

Studies have shown that humility is one of the most important characteristics of successful leaders. A leadership expert wrote in *Forbes* magazine that "humble leaders listen more effectively, inspire great teamwork, and focus everyone (including themselves) on organizational goals."[19]

George Washington and Ronald Reagan are textbook examples of that description.

Historians have noted that General Washington's humility set him apart from other legendary generals throughout history.[20] Alexander the Great, George S. Patton, Genghis Khan, Napoleon Bonaparte, and many others are notable for their strategy, ferocity, and commanding presence, but they might also be remembered for their arrogance and sense of superiority.

> *The leader's strongest tool is humility. It intensifies credibility.*
> —John Dickson

Washington, on the other hand, was selfless. He served without pay. He put the safety and well-being of his men above all else, and he let them know he respected and cared about them. He shared their severe hardships. American military historian Edward G. Lengel observed that Washington endured the bitterly cold winter of 1777–78 at

Valley Forge with his regiments: "He did not take leave, as many officers did, and it was common knowledge that he spared no effort to keep the men housed, fed, and warm."[21] Is it any wonder that his soldiers and fellow Americans would follow him into battle?

David McCullough, the Pulitzer Prize–winning author of *John Adams* and *Truman*, wrote that General Washington avoided catastrophic mistakes by listening to the advice of his war council and messengers who reported to him. He had no ego; he took counsel from anyone who had good ideas.

Historian Michael Stallard wrote that Washington "was known as a listener who considered others' views. During the Constitutional Convention over which he presided, Washington rarely said a word other than to intervene and make decisions to break a logjam in the deliberations."[22]

Like President Washington, President Reagan seemed to innately understand that a good leader places his entire attention on preserving the people's right to life, liberty, and the pursuit of happiness—whatever that may mean to each human being. But while Reagan focused on the nation as a whole, he never forgot the individual. I witnessed many small acts of kindness and civility during my time in service to him.

I developed a TEDx talk around an experience I call my "After You" story. My White House colleague Joanne Drake, now chief administrative officer for the Reagan Library Foundation, has a similar story to tell about Ronald Reagan. We experienced the same genuine man time after time. Sometimes I would escort President Reagan to an event. When we reached an elevator, he always insisted I enter first. I'd say, "Mr. President, after you." He'd reply, "Oh, no! After *you*!" with a warm smile and twinkling eyes. Such a powerful leader could easily have ignored me and walked into the elevator first, but President Reagan showed me respect, and I am honored by his gracious act. He was the most powerful, influential leader in the world, yet he had the humility to notice me and let me go first.

When I left the White House to work at the State Department protocol office, I was honored to bid farewell to President Reagan in the Oval Office in a "one on one." (There's actually a video of it floating around the internet—a little embarrassing since I fawned over him, but I meant every word I said and will remember the experience forever.) At the end of that special meeting, he presented me with a replica of the plaque displayed on his desk:

> There is no limit to what a man can do or where he can go, as long as he does not care who gets the credit.[23]

I took those words to heart, although sometimes it can be hard to live up to such an ideal. I often reflect on Reagan's example of humility and generosity of spirit. He was an extraordinary human being and larger than life—a former movie star, governor of California, and ultimately leader of the free world—but he treated everyone with respect and courtesy and made everyone feel valued. He was not falsely modest—Reagan was aware of his exceptional gifts, his purpose, and his significant role in history—but he was, deep to his core, a gracious and humble man.

> *Humility is the only true wisdom by which we prepare our minds for all the possible changes of life.*
> —George Arliss

Think of other great leaders: Martin Luther King Jr., Gandhi, Mother Teresa, Nelson Mandela, Abraham Lincoln. None of them believed they were more important than their messages, nor more valuable than those who followed them. They engaged, empowered, and inspired others because they were humble. They lived to be in service to others. They did not seek credit or admiration for their work, but neither were they weak or passive. Their humility supported a boundless strength of character that created the environment for so many people to trust in them, believe in their causes, and help them achieve their goals.

One of the most approachable leaders I had the pleasure of working with was Nelson Mandela. My friend Bill Sittmann (may he rest in peace) was the executive secretariat at the National Security Council in the George H. W. Bush White House. Nelson Mandela had been recently released from his long prison term in South Africa. I had just started my business, Practical Protocol, so Bill referred me to the group organizing Mr. Mandela's visit to the United States. They hired me to organize the visits to the White House, the State Department, and Capitol Hill.

> *As I have said, the first thing is to be honest with yourself. You can never have an impact on society if you have not changed yourself. [...] Great peacemakers are all people of integrity [and] honesty, but [also] humility.*
>
> —**Nelson Mandela**

It was a tremendous honor and incredible opportunity to spend just a little time with *the* Nelson Mandela. Was he as advertised? Absolutely. Charming, kind, soft-spoken, and very approachable—in a word, humble. Even then I could feel how lucky I was to have the chance to work for and to serve such amazing individuals. I was deeply humbled in the process.

Ego, Step Aside

I personally came to appreciate the tremendous value of approachability after coming to terms with a part of my ego that was getting in the way. Even sharing this personal experience makes me feel as if I am failing in the humility arena, but here goes.

> *We can measure our servant's heart when others treat us like servants. How do you react when you're taken for granted, bossed around, or treated as an inferior?*
>
> —*Rick Warren*

I am often approached by people I don't know. If I'm on a plane and I walk down the aisle, I'm asked for coffee refills. In shopping centers and restaurants, I've had people ask where they might find the loo (bathroom). In clothing stores, customers ask me if an item of clothing is available in a different size. When I was younger, I recoiled somewhat at such requests. I was a bit insulted at the thought that someone would take me for the flight attendant or store employee. After all, I was *such* a fancy (albeit young) career woman. I am afraid I was not very humble.

A close friend suggested that perhaps these things happened because I seemed like an approachable person, that people might have thought I looked like someone who could be trusted to help them. There was truly an aha moment. Rather than take umbrage at the requests, I shifted my thinking then and there. From that point forward, I wanted to be that person: approachable and helpful—like Mandela.

Now I am incredibly flattered someone would feel comfortable approaching me and asking for help. Coffee? Right away. Size eight? Let's go find out. A new fork? Of course! Some of the best conversations ensue when people realize I am actually *not* an employee of the establishment. I have met some interesting people because of my willingness to help. The reward is in the service. It has actually become a favorite, very satisfying part of my practice of civility.

My friend John Walsh, a business partner in a variety of intriguing enterprises, showed me his humility early on. I think it's one of the reasons I trust and respect him so much. We had a company called Tech-Knowledge International, which hosted foreign trade missions with delegations headed by ministers of energy, health, transportation, and so on. He could host a substantive meeting with the minister and the head of a hospital or major company and then jump right into making sure that the delegation's luggage was properly delivered. He treated VIPs and their teams with equal dignity and respect. He never saw himself above helping someone. In fact, it's what he values most: helping others, especially children. He has plenty of self-confidence that comes from his experience, but he puts his ego aside more often than not. That, to me, exemplifies the quintessential servant-leader.

Humility Is Quiet, Thoughtful, and Civil

Sometimes we learn about a quality by witnessing the effect of its absence. Defense attorney Robert (Bob) Bennett, who defended famous and infamous clients, gave me an example of how the lack of humility is counterproductive:

> When I was doing more civil litigation than I do now, every now and then, I'd run into a plaintiff's lawyer who felt that to impress his client, he had to be nasty. I thought it was very counterproductive. The end result for me was

that I was turned off. I just said, "Fine with you. When you get civil, we can talk."

Now sometimes clients want that and expect that. They feel to get their money's worth they have to have someone who's pounding the table. But over time, I found that to be most ineffective. You know, you can say *no* in a nice, quiet, civil way. You don't have to bang the table.[24]

Have you ever had an experience in your work life in which you chose to "bang the table" and assert that your opinion is more important than others'? I know I have. We're only human, after all—sometimes our tempers and egos get the better of us. As Dr. Phil would say, "How did that work for you?" Did you find, like Bennett, that a quiet, humble approach might have worked better?

Hubris versus Humility

We might think that humility is the opposite of hubris (excessive pride or self-confidence; arrogance that ultimately leads to a downfall). However, we can think of humility as the ballast or center of a seesaw. Humility balances out the extreme characteristics of hubris and lack of self-worth. We are at our best selves when we understand that we are "not nothing" but rather that we are "not everything"! We are just one part of a larger part of the infinite.

"Leaders tainted by hubris give life to toxic environments, workplaces where incivility and downright hostility often flourish," wrote leadership guru Audrey Murrell.²⁵ However, the reverse can also be true, she noted:

> Leaders who choose humility, and who model humbleness in their actions, create the opposite kind of environment. This environment is grounded in respect, tolerance, and outcomes that are mutually beneficial for the firm and for the individual.

People with hubris arrogantly believe that their way is the only way and that they are the only ones who know how to accomplish something. Shakespeare's *Macbeth* is a classic literary example of hubris and its consequences. Today, we might point to the despicable Jeffrey Epstein as the ultimate symbol of hubris. He and those he collaborated with thought themselves untouchable. We see what became of him. As of this writing, we have not yet witnessed the inevitable downfall of all those associated with him. There will be a price to pay for hubris—there always is.

Many people believe that humility is the opposite of pride, when in fact it is a point of equilibrium. The opposite of pride is actually a lack of self-esteem. A humble person is totally different from a person who cannot recognize and appreciate himself as part of this world's marvels.

—attributed to Rabino Nilton Bonder

On the eve of his Declaration of Emancipation in 1863, Abraham Lincoln told his cabinet that someone else might do a better job as president:

> I know very well that many others might, in this matter, as in others, do better than I can; and if I was satisfied that the public confidence was more fully possessed by any one

of them than by me, and knew of any constitutional way in which he could be put in my place, he should have it.[26]

Lincoln's humility did not mean that he shrugged his shoulders and let someone else take the reins or that he lacked self-worth. "However, this may be," Lincoln said, "there is no way in which I can have any other put where I am. I am here. I must do the best I can and bear the responsibility of taking the course which I feel I ought to take."

Humility doesn't require us to abandon our self-confidence; Lincoln was not insecure, and he knew he was up to the task. But he respected and appreciated the strengths of others, and always sought the counsel of his cabinet before making a significant decision.

On the occasions when I was too aggressive, impatient, defensive, or angry in my professional work, I tended to overlook an essential priority: respect for others. Every single time, I've rued not taking a softer, humbler approach.

I remember well one time in particular, and I will always regret my behavior that day. I was working on the Desert Storm Parade Committee and had about eight direct reports. One was in charge of the families of those who were killed in action (KIA). Something had gone awry in the planning, and the KIA families weren't being treated as well as I thought they should. After all, they are the ones who sacrificed the most in Operation Desert Storm; their loved ones had given their lives in service to our country.

I scolded the responsible person in front of the rest of the committee. Immediately afterward, I knew I had been wrong to handle it publicly, and I really hope that I apologized. While the position on the issue I was railing about may have been reason-

> *Pride is concerned with who is right. Humility is concerned with what is right.*
> —Ezra Taft Benson

able, the way I handled it was not. A humble, thoughtful leader would have spoken to the person privately and would have asked them questions to help them discover and own their mistake. Then we could move to find a solution together. Giving in to that bit of temper and allowing my sense of self-righteousness to take over—my conviction that I was right—might have helped me vent my frustration in the short term, but it didn't help the staffer do anything to fix the overall problem. Instead, if I had been a truly humble leader, I would have first considered my own management failings instead of hammering my colleague on his. All these years later, I cringe a little as I remember that moment. I can only hope that the staff member and the witnesses to my hubris-driven behavior do not.

Anita McBride, Executive in Residence at the School of Public Affairs at American University, was chief of staff to former First Lady Laura Bush during the George W. Bush presidency. She told me a story about Mrs. Bush that illustrates great humility.[27]

In the 2004 presidential campaign, Senator John Kerry was running against President Bush. His wife, Teresa Heinz Kerry, was asked in an interview what the difference was between her and the First Lady, and in response she made a comment about Laura Bush that some considered demeaning: "I don't know if she's ever had a real job." Of course, it caused a stir. The media would have liked nothing more than to fuel a fight between the two.

Instead of taking the bait, Mrs. Bush completely defused the situation with a gracious response: "It didn't hurt my feelings. She didn't have to apologize—I know how tough it is. And actually, I know those trick questions."

Mrs. Bush didn't let her pride or ego get in the way; she chose humility and grace instead of being offended by a condescending remark. Her example taught me to give people the benefit of the doubt, and that even in the throes of political gamesmanship, we can take the high road.

Humility and "Win-Wins" versus Playing a Zero-Sum Game

The D.C. lobbying industry isn't the most popular these days. Still, one special lobbyist garnered a place in the book *Politics with Principle: Ten Characters with Character*, by Michael Kerrigan. Charlie Black, cofounder of the first bipartisan lobbying firm in Washington, D.C., is an exceptionally humble man. Getting win-wins isn't easy anywhere, especially in the current and prolonged division and volatility of the political climate in our nation's capital. Charlie certainly has his work cut out for him. He's been working in D.C. for almost half a century, mostly in politics and government relations.

"I used to hear stories in the old days," he says, "about smoke-filled rooms and arm-twisting, and that doesn't work. If it ever did, it doesn't work anymore. We have a firm with about half Republicans and half Democrats, and that allows us to provide full service to the clients. You can't get anything important done without bipartisan support."[28]

Charlie's words give me hope. We keep hearing the downside of Washington politics. Every day in the news, we're hit with a story about the fighting going on, not only across the aisle but also within the parties themselves. Maybe progress on the Hill is extremely slow, but if bipartisan support is required for anything important to get done, doesn't that fact hint at the significance of civility? Isn't that reason enough for us to go full throttle on a civility movement?

I'm grateful that influential and humble people in D.C. recognize that win-wins are essential for our country to thrive. How do we remove ego and politics from the equation and find common ground? Right now, it seems impossible. If ever there were a man whose humility will let him accomplish win-wins in Congress, it's Charlie Black.

Some business and organizational processes also focus on collaboration and seeking win-wins. "Design Thinking," a process originally used in engineering and product innovation, is becoming more commonplace in mainstream business-process innovation. I'm in love with this way of reinventing something! I think the reason it resonates with me is because of the way it requires input from other people and is such a positive, civil way of taking something apart and putting it back together again.

Solving problems via Design Thinking methodology allows for ingenuity, brilliance, and those aha moments of discovery, but it also requires team members to look at the world through a child's eyes, with the blissful naivete of not knowing something won't work. It is intellectual humility demanding an open mind and open heart. Perhaps Design Thinking can be put to work to bring civility to our society, to take our current ideologies apart and put them back together in a positive way, instead of taking a burn-it-all-down approach, which seems so destructive.

HUMILITY THROUGH A RELIGIOUS LENS

Just as the Golden Rule presents itself in just about every religion, so, too, does humility appear as a central tenet in most religious philosophies.

In Christianity, Judaism, Buddhism, Hinduism, and Greek mythology, to name just a few religions and philosophies, we learn that humility is not a weakness but a great strength. Meek is not weak. In the New Testament, for example, Jesus said, "Blessed are the meek: for they shall inherit the earth."[29] He also described himself as "meek and lowly of heart."[30] I interpret the word *meek* in these examples as meaning "humble."

> *He who offers humility unto God and man shall be rewarded with a reward as if he had offered all the sacrifices in the world.*
>
> —The Talmud

One Christian leader gave his interpretation of what Jesus meant: "He was saying that only those who are humble enough to forgo the vain glories of the world and to follow the paths of righteousness [. . .] will possess the earth."[31] In other words, "the meek" (or humble) are those who are respectful and willing to subdue their will to God's. To become humble, "one must constantly be reminded of his dependence [. . .] on the Lord."[32]

In Spanish, the word *meek* is translated as *manso*. But *manso* is also the adjective used for "tame"—which is closer to the biblical ideal. Elayne Wells Harmer, my friend and editor, was born in Argentina. She shared an experience that illustrates the relationship between the nuanced concept of being "tame" and being humble.

Her father, Robert, a Christian missionary, once visited a hundred-thousand-acre ranch in the lush pampas of Argentina, where the owner raised grass-fed beef. His hobby was raising and training thoroughbred horses to be used for racing and polo and by the expert gauchos (cowboys) on the ranch. The owner had more than a thousand of these beautiful animals, each with its pedigree and each well trained—or in the process of becoming so. The ranch's reputation was such that there was a demand for its horses at premium prices all over the world.

Robert asked the ranch owner if he could see a rodeo like they had in the western part of the United States, where the cowboys "break" horses.

The owner was aghast. "Not on this ranch, you won't!" he said emphatically in Spanish. "Our horses have to be lightning fast, fearless, and courageous on the playing field, instantly obedient to every hint of a command and superbly maneuverable. We would never 'break' a horse like you Yankee cowboys! We don't want to break their spirit. We love our horses, and we work patiently with them until they are *manso*."

Robert interpreted *manso* as meek or humble, so he was confused. The ranch owner clarified. "*Manso* horses are full of fire and spirit, but they are tame, respectful, and well trained," he explained.

Robert often applied the insight he gained from that conversation to his sermons. After that experience, he taught that Jesus did not mean for us to be doormats—he certainly wasn't one. Instead, Jesus meant that we should be obedient and respectful of God and well trained or educated. "We can be strong, enthusiastic, talented, spirited, zealous, and bold and still be 'meek' or humble," Robert would say.

In Buddhism, humility is one of the ten sacred qualities attributed to the Buddha of Compassion. A professor of religious studies in Taiwan explained that humility comes when a practitioner "transcends all worldly desires, illusions, and mental constructs and labels associated with the ego."[33] Buddhists believe that humility is demonstrated by respecting others, showing a genuine human interest in them, and recognizing that "our biological self is fraught with frailties and ignorance and that a true self is characterized by such divine qualities as love, compassion, joy, and wisdom innate in every one of us."[34]

Hindus use a parable to illustrate humility: when rice paddy crops begin to bear grains, they bend, and when the grains are ripe, they bend farther. The more grain, the greater they incline toward the ground. Likewise, the branches of mango trees laden with fruits bend down because of the weight of the fruits. In this allegory, the grain or the heavy fruit is knowledge, and the bending toward the ground is humility. The more experience one has and the more one knows, the more one should be humble and realize how much there is still to learn. The *gnani* (one who is educated or knowledgeable) is humble because of his wisdom, said Hindu chieftain Malayaman. Because humility goes hand in hand with self-control, explained a Hindu writer, "a *gnani* will never be impressed by words of praise or hurt by words of criticism. He will act according to dharma.[35] He who is not moved by praise will not be led astray by flattery."[36]

HUMILITY AS A FORM OF GRATITUDE

The outward and deliberate expression of gratitude to others helps make us less self-focused. A recent study found that gratitude and humility are self-reinforcing. If we are truly grateful, we receive an understanding of our place in the mix of all humanity. Offering our best qualities to the world while honoring those of others can humble us and help dissipate the destructive energies that are taking up so much space in the world. Humility doesn't care about winning points, keeping score, or seeking approval from any outside source. The same can be said of the civil life in general: civility isn't about getting credit for doing the right thing. To me, it's about developing

> *When you are older, you will know that life is a long lesson in humility.*
> —James M. Barrie

character and integrity that resolutely reside within us and then listening to that inner voice, our conscience. If we do this, with none the wiser, we succeed in exhibiting what I now consider *the* core component of civility: humility.

CHAPTER SIX

Empathy

Show nothing to your friend that may affright him.

—Rule 3

Be no flatterer, neither play with any that delights not to be played withal.

—Rule 17

Show not yourself glad at the misfortune of another, though he were your enemy.

—Rule 22

Do not express joy before one sick or in pain, for that contrary passion will aggravate his misery.

—Rule 43

Perhaps second only to humility in our quest for genuine civility is the ability to empathize. Referring back to the OED, empathy is "the power of projecting one's personality into (and thus fully comprehending) the object of contemplation."[37]

In 2011, my friend Jessica Buchanan was a USAID* worker teaching in Somalia when she and a Danish coworker were kidnapped and held for ransom. Through torture, neglect, and abuse, she made a decision that while her body was captive, they could not hold her mind hostage. She kept herself mentally healthy by remembering the most minute details of her life. Once she relived each memory of her past, she started imagining every detail of her future when she would be home again: her husband, the children she would have, what her life would look like. These mental images are what kept her going, despite the abysmal state of her physical health.

On day ninety-three of Jessica's captivity, President Obama sent SEAL Team Six to execute a rescue mission. Today she lives a happy, fulfilled life in northern Virginia with her husband and two children. While her long journey to complete recovery continues to this day, her story is one of true courage, perseverance, and grace.

While we can feel sympathy and tremendous sadness for what Jessica endured, how can we *ever* empathize with her? Most of us has never been remotely close to having such a harrowing experience—and thank goodness for that! Fearing for your life every day for ninety-three days leaves an indelible impression. Fortunately, for most of us, even enduring the COVID-19 pandemic is nowhere near as traumatic as Jessica's trial.

But perhaps this global plague that affected virtually every corner of the world can help us empathize with Jessica. All around the world, the pandemic became extremely scary and frighteningly

---

* United States Agency for International Development.

real. No one knew what would come next or how it would unfold. We all did our personal best to minimize the effects of the virus on our immediate community and society as a whole, without knowing when it would end or where it would lead. As of the date of publication, we still don't know.

Jessica did not know what was coming. Would she find death at the hands of her captors or from deteriorating health? Would she see liberation and freedom? She just did not know. The fear of the unknown can lead to stress, anxiety, and mental and physical health challenges. Due to COVID-19, we *can* relate to that, can't we? Using our imagination to try to understand what someone else might be feeling is doable. We just need to *want* to feel.

Some years ago, Jessica was hiking with her family in Shenandoah National Park when she had an epiphany about empathy. When they stopped for a water break, some people passed them. They appeared to be a big family—about ten of them, from babies to a granny. One of the men carried a shovel, which they thought was strange. A little while later, when they continued hiking, they saw the family off the trail in a particularly beautiful area. As they slowed down, they saw the man take out a container from his backpack and throw the contents into the air. It was clear from the family's reverence that he was releasing the ashes of someone they loved, and it was a tender, memorable experience.

We never know what someone might be carrying around with them, do we? Kindness and compassion and as much empathy as we can muster toward friends and strangers alike will bring us closer to one another, because even the most "together" person deals with something. We all have *something* in our "backpack" that is difficult to carry and not always apparent to anyone but ourselves.

The Age of Empathy

After many years of studying social behavior in herd animals like elephants and chimpanzees, contemporary primatologist Frans de Waal concluded that both animals and humans are wired to help.[38] His theory contradicts the common wisdom that humans instinctively put themselves first.

He illustrates his point by looking at Hurricane Katrina relief efforts as a pivotal point in our society's development. Americans were outraged and shocked by the images of human corpses floating in the streets of New Orleans, while local, state, and federal government officials argued about who was in charge of rescue and recovery. While politicians and government agencies bickered, ordinary people from across the country contributed time, money, and resources to help New Orleans.

Through their actions, these people showed that they loved and cared for their fellow humans, bureaucratic tape be damned. They demonstrated civility to one another. Their service belied the criticism that humans are inherently selfish or indifferent to the plights of others.

Sadly, when the crisis was over, people generally retreated back into their own worlds, and political squabbling resumed unabated. But de Waal insists that a precedent was set during Katrina. Never again, he says, will our country allow such a time gap between a crisis and helping people. The "age of empathy," as de Waal calls it, was born during that devastating hurricane, and the vocabulary of empathy became part of the social discourse.

The Power of EQ to Increase Civil Behavior

Peter Salovey and John D. Mayer coined the term *emotional intelligence* in 1990, describing it as "the ability to monitor one's own and other people's emotions [. . .] and to use emotional information to guide thinking and behavior."[39] Later, Daniel Goleman, PhD, authored the worldwide bestseller *Working with Emotional Intelligence*.

There's an important distinction between EQ (emotional quotient) and IQ (intelligence quotient): We can increase EQ, while IQ generally remains the same throughout our lives. We can engage in practical techniques that can raise our EQ and thereby raise our ability to build a strong practice of civility.

Radio host and entrepreneur Abhi Golhar details ten ways to increase your emotional intelligence. I've summarized and combined them into eight points:

1. Use an assertive (direct) style of communicating, while still respecting the feelings of others.

2. *Respond* to conflict instead of *reacting* to it. Keep in mind that the goal is to seek resolution, so make sure your words and actions are in alignment with that objective.

3. Use active listening skills. Don't just wait for the chance to respond—show respect by really listening, and let the person finish expressing their thoughts.

4. Practice self-awareness and ways to maintain a positive attitude. Active awareness of our moods and the emotional state of others helps us adjust negative attitudes.

5. Take criticism well. Take a moment to understand where it's coming from, and try to constructively resolve issues.

6. Empathize with others. Empathy creates a space for mutual respect, where positive conversations can occur between people of differing opinions.

7. Use positive leadership skills. Take the initiative, make good decisions, and increase your ability to solve problems.

8. Be approachable and sociable. Interpersonal skills help you communicate clearly.[40]

Empathy at Work

According to a 2018 State of the Workplace Empathy study, 96 percent believed empathy was an important quality for the leadership of a company.[41] In an increase over previous years, 92 percent of those same respondents felt that empathy in their company is still undervalued.

The message is that employers who value empathy and promote an empathetic work environment can increase the happiness quotient inside their company, which translates into quantifiable gains in productivity and reduces costly turnover. In a post-COVID-19, remote- and distance-work world, the need to nurture a compassionate company environment is more important than ever.

We are all too aware that cash is the bottom line of any business, that money makes the world go around. But in settling into the "new normal," we must also understand what the practice of empathy and civility can do to help an out-of-sorts workforce feel stable and able to focus on the work at hand.

There is a phenomenon known as "compassion fatigue." According to the Compassion Fatigue Awareness Project, this occurrence is "a broadly defined concept that can include emotional, physical, and spiritual distress in those providing care to another. It is associated with caregiving where people or animals are experiencing significant emotional or physical pain and suffering."[42]

> *One often reads about the art of conversation [...] but wouldn't you agree that the infinitely more valuable rara avis is a good listener?*
> —*Malcolm Forbes*

I've concluded that the solution is a bit like putting on our own oxygen masks on a plane before we help anyone else. We are unable to be of service to others if we ourselves have no oxygen.

Listening Leads to Empathy

In a letter of advice to a young writer, Ernest Hemingway wrote, "When people talk, listen completely. Most people never listen."[43] I've learned that listening well is an art, and in an ongoing practice of civility, it's an integral step to developing empathy. I work at it all the time.

Let's remember that when we approach someone whose views differ from our own, instead of attacking or cross-examining, we can ask open-ended, sincere questions: How did you come to feel that way? Can you share some examples so I can get a better idea of your experiences? Then we need to *listen*.

Note that I said we need to approach *them*. We need to show leadership, swallow our pride, and be the one to open the conversation by asking to hear *their* point of view. Let's make it clear we're listening and respecting them—not just waiting to get our opinion out. When we listen to another human being speaking to us, we're showing respect for that person's feelings and their ideas. We're saying they matter.

Pakistani novelist Mohsin Hamid said, "Empathy is about finding echoes of another person in yourself."[44] Hamid expresses beautifully what civility is about: recognizing the humanity of our fellow earth dwellers. It's about walking that mile in their shoes. Empathy makes it possible for us to find common ground and, from there, possibly a relationship.

Empathy-Based Listening

At 5:00 a.m. on December 13, 2003, Delta Force member Eric Maddox began interrogating Mohammed Ibrahim Omar al-Muslit, Saddam Hussein's bodyguard. The Americans had nicknamed al-Muslit "the Ace of Spades" for his close relationship to Saddam. Maddox believed the man in front of him knew where the Iraqi leader was hiding, and it was up to him to get Omar al-Muslit to spill.

Prior to this interrogation, Maddox had been using a unique technique he called "empathy-based listening" with other prisoners. He dropped his preconceived ideas and biases and listened to the men's stories. "They needed to be heard," Maddox said, "and

> *When I really see you, I think something changes on my face. [...] I think it's a dynamic interaction. You're changed by how I'm changed. And we have a much better chance at getting together on what we're talking about.*
>
> —*Alan Alda*

when they were heard, they opened up."[45] The prisoners started trusting him, giving up information and negotiating with him to make deals. When Maddox listened to al-Muslit and *then* questioned him, the bodyguard offered up the information that led to Saddam's hiding place.

"Put yourselves in the shoes of the person you're talking to," Maddox said. "That's empathy."[46]

Now, with the exception of true sociopaths, most humans innately understand the concept of empathy. However, what does empathy do to or for us? How does it help or contribute to a practice of civility? Empathetic people have the ability to look at the world through another's eyes; it's being sensitive enough to understand what someone else sees and feels.

According to Maddox, to gain empathy we must "remove [our] mental distractions and seek exclusively to understand the situation from the other person's perspective—without any bias, agenda, or personal goals."[47] But in fact, Maddox did have an agenda. He wanted to know where Saddam Hussein was hiding, and he needed to build trust and rapport with the man who knew the answer. But he knew that succeeding in his quest required him to separate his ego from the task at hand and earnestly get to know the man sitting in front of him. Eventually their conversation led them right to the rabbit-hole hiding place of Saddam Hussein.

As I asked earlier, what benefit do we receive from expressing, creating, and developing empathy for another person? Our neurological "joy juices" are ignited, and we feel good—plain and simple. And what benefit does the recipient of that empathy receive? It ignites the same joy and builds a feeling of trust between the parties, so much so that a collaborator with a terrorist dictator bonded with his interrogator.

Respect is tied to our ability to listen to other people's concerns. It's only through listening that we can learn what people are thinking, so it's imperative that we become good listeners.

Will Rogers, famous humorist, social commentator, and a good friend of my grandfather Jimmie Mattern, once said, "Never miss a good chance to shut up." It's good advice. It stuck with me the first time I read it, and now I think of it all the time when I'm in a conversation with other people. It keeps me humble and (hopefully) listening.

Playing Ball

Sean Mahar, coauthor of the 2020 book *Stop Wasting Words* and founder of a consulting and coaching organization on critical conversations, compares human communication to a game of catch. One person throws the ball; the other catches. In a good game, throwing and catching don't happen simultaneously. Mahar explains that a good pitcher throws the ball in a way that allows the catcher to actually catch it. Obvious, right?

Think of how often we pitch, throw, and hurl words that won't be "caught" or received well. If we seek real connection, it's important to make sure we're talking to be *understood* instead of talking to get our best "pitch" in. We need to make sure the listener is ready to "catch" what we're saying, and we need to give the catcher the same courtesy.

Not everyone thinks empathy is always a good thing. Yale psychology professor Paul Bloom draws a distinction between empathy—which he defines as feeling another's experience, including pain—and compassion and kindness.[48] While he is all for compassion and kindness, Bloom believes that sometimes our prejudices cause us to feel empathy more for one group of people over another. He believes "empathy bias" can lead to ills such as tribalism, racism, discrimination, and even violence and war. Bloom suggests we stick to reason when it comes to figuring out how to help make the world a better place for our fellow humans.[49]

I'd like to use his provocative point to fine-tune our own understanding of and commitment to empathy. Yes, we all come from different backgrounds and experiences, and we might naturally feel more emotion-based empathy for a person or group we understand than a person or group with whom or with which we've had no experience. But can we not counter our inherent tendency to aid people we "get" by becoming aware of that impulse? Because we are now in an age where there is such polarity and splintering into different identity communities, it's time to be extra brave and reach out to people with whom we seemingly have little in common.

EMPATHY AND VULNERABILITY

Dr. Brené Brown, research professor at the University of Houston and the author of five number-one *New York Times* nonfiction bestsellers, has heard a lot of the latest talk on how empathy might not always be a good thing. Some people say that when we show empathy, we are taking on someone else's darkness, which can lead to undue stress and burnout. OK, I'd like to avoid that! But Brown has an interesting way of looking at it. She sees empathy as a skill set used to manifest compassion, or deep love for other people so they know they're not alone. In other words, empathy is a tool we can turn on or off, put away or take out to use. It doesn't have to overwhelm us, no matter how desperate or sad the situation:

> Empathy is [...] about how to communicate that deep love for people, in a way so that people know they're not alone. But empathy is not feeling *for* somebody. It's feeling *with* them. It's touching a place in me that knows where you've been, so I can look at you and say, 'Me, too, brother. You're not alone in this.'[50]

Empathy isn't like opening a big sack, stuffing a heavy load of the entire world's problems into it, and lugging it on your back—it's something you can carry with you lightly. It doesn't have to sap us of energy or weigh us down. It's simply being with someone in their suffering—or their joy. We can be *with* someone, no matter how they are experiencing their life, without getting sucked into a vortex of pain and suffering.

Empathy keeps giving back to us. The more empathy we show, the more connection, and thus joy, we feel, which doesn't make sense when a lot of the time we're empathizing with people's suffering. Joy comes from sitting alongside a person, showing the person we care, and knowing that for that moment, our life has a very strong purpose.

Times are such that if we each try, in a humble, sincere way, to empathize with those we don't sense we have a lot in common with, we might make a real difference *now*, instead of later. With each of us facing the truth of our myriad polarities yet showing the fortitude to take action to "be with" someone in their struggle, we can start to bring true civility to our world.

I spoke with my friend Meryl Chertoff, executive director of the Georgetown Project on State and Local Government Policy and Law at Georgetown University, about civility when she ran the Justice and Society program for the Aspen Institute. For a conversation to be deemed "successful," she said, both parties must come out feeling better than when they started talking. Meryl shared some helpful tips on how we can engage in more productive dialogue:

> Some of the most destructive conversations are when we label or denigrate people. We "other" them. Rather than "othering," it's empathy that helps us ask ourselves: "Where is the other person coming from? What experiences are they bringing to this conversation? What prejudices or biases are present? And what do I really need to do in order to make this a productive interaction?"[51]

Meryl talked about the word *namaste*, often used in yoga and as a greeting in many parts of India. It translates to "I see the divine within you." Meryl notes that whether we see divinity or simply humanity in another person, we must "truly see the other person and recognize their goodness."

President Washington displayed immense courage to change the status quo. Robert F. Kennedy Jr. noted that despite the British Army's despicable treatment of captured American soldiers, General Washington considered "the decent treatment of enemy combatants to be one of the principal strategic preoccupations of the American Revolution."[52] When his own soldiers were taken prisoner by the British and Germans, many of them were shown little to no mercy—they were either severely mistreated or even killed. But Washington wanted to show the world how a democratic society rises above such cruelties. He made the choice to recognize the humanity in his enemies and commanded his troops to treat prisoners with dignity and kindness.

Following the Golden Rule

Part of empathy is understanding the concept of reciprocal kindness and compassion referred to as the Golden Rule: Treat others the way we want others to treat us. Although it is widely considered a biblical decree, every world religion or philosophy has a variation.*

These rules are close to the heart of every civil person: think of the people around you, show empathy to your fellow man, and treat everyone kindly. We know how to because it's how we all want to be treated. It's so simple in concept, but so easy to forget. The iconic artist Norman Rockwell, who depicted homey American scenes for *The Saturday Evening Post*, once created a painting that was a bit out of his usual wheelhouse. He wanted to depict people of all races, cultures, and religions as unified in pursuit of peace and happiness and treating each other with courtesy and respect. The painting includes this phrase: *Do unto others as you would have them do unto you.*

"Not always the same words," Rockwell said, "but the same idea."[53]

The painting is not specifically about American culture, yet in a larger sense it is, because we are a vast melting pot of different cultures, races, ethnicities, and personalities. Former First Lady Nancy Reagan commissioned a mosaic re-creation of the painting and donated it to the United Nations on behalf of the United States. It is still on display at the UN's headquarters in New York.

If we are to combat the seemingly constant stream of uncivil behavior on social media, on TV screens, and in our own towns and neighborhoods, we should consider practicing the Golden Rule more than ever before: love our neighbors as we do ourselves.

---

* For a sample, see "Variations of the Golden Rule" on page 141.

At times when we feel unfairly treated, remember this: "Nothing in the Golden Rule says that others will treat us as we have treated them. It only says that we must treat others in a way that *we* would want to be treated."[54] Another phrase that helps me remember to be kind when I face inevitable frustrations in human interactions is this: "They may forget what you said, but they will never forget how you made them feel."[55]

I had an experience many years ago that I will never forget. Around 1987, I was asked to accompany a young Soviet embassy official around the State Department while his boss, the Soviet ambassador, was meeting with then Secretary of State George Shultz. After all, we couldn't leave the official unattended to wander about the place. His name was David Chikvaidze. Somehow he got away from me (probably for a smoke), but I found him walking back into the main entrance of the State Department, and we began to chat. What started out as a babysitting job became a friendship.

I lost track of David again, but years later I discovered him working in Geneva as the Chef de Cabinet for the director-general of the United Nations Office at Geneva (UNOG). Whenever I go to Geneva now, I look him up. One year, he took my nephew Jack and me to the Independence Day party at the U.S. Embassy. In our last visit in his offices in Geneva, we chatted about the importance of relationships as it relates to civility and international diplomacy. I'm paraphrasing what he said to me then:

> You know what was important? We trusted each other. When there were problems, we resolved them. Very often, the solution was based on each of us doing the legwork, inside your administration or my embassy. Because like any big organization, you have to navigate it. You have to advocate as facilitators. That's why we established a camaraderie. I mean, you are here today exactly thirty years

after meeting. We're talking as old friends. Why? Because we trusted each other from that time. I'm not sure that Russian and American officials of whatever level today have that kind of a relationship.

In his autobiography, John D. Rockefeller wrote that "a friendship founded on business is a good deal better than a business founded on friendship." The friendship that David and I developed was based on business and on trust. It was better than business, because there was no commercial interest on either side. We were working in the same direction.

That's what David tries to do day in and day out at the UN. On behalf of the director general, he works to get the 176 missions out of 193 member states moving in the same direction. He's a troubleshooter, a problem solver, an honest broker. I'm grateful he's in that role and part of an effort to create a space for civility.

An Evolutionary Need for Connection

The Smithsonian Institution in Washington, D.C., holds an annual Folklife Festival on the National Mall, bringing together tradition bearers and exemplars from three different cultures. Before COVID-19, about a million people visited the festival. In 2008, the three different "cultures" were the National Aeronautics and Space Administration (NASA), the roots of Texas music and food, and the tiny mountain kingdom of Bhutan.

Nicole Krakora, then director of special events and protocol at the Smithsonian, recalls what a daunting task it was to find a connection between the disparate cultures:

We had cowboys, Buddhist monks, and astronauts, and I am wondering how in the world are we going to find anything in common. Well, it happened immediately. I was backstage at the opening ceremony, and we had the governor of Texas, the prince of Bhutan, and the administrator of NASA.

There was a musician from Bhutan who didn't speak any English. He had never left his village, let alone his country. His instrument was a *dramyin*—a six-string lute—and it was beautifully painted. Then here comes a couple cowboys from Texas. One with his guitar and another with a banjo. They did not speak Bhutanese. But they all recognized what made them alike. They recognized their similar instruments and started playing together. Then they started trading instruments and teaching each other how to play. No talking, just smiles.

It was magic. The magic of music to bring people together to find their common humanity. If you just have your eyes open, it can be pretty delightful—there can still be a sense of wonder about the world and the coming together of seemingly disparate cultures.[56]

From an evolutionary perspective, we're hardwired to connect to other people. Scientist Matthew Lieberman, author of a book on the neuroscience of human connection, wrote, "Becoming more socially connected is essential to our survival. In a sense, evolution has made bets at each step that the best way to make us more successful is to make us more social."[57] He explains that the physical pain we feel at being excluded or even heartbroken is very real, because we have an essential need to connect with other people, the same way we require oxygen and water:

> Data suggests that we [. . .] suffer greatly when our social bonds are threatened or severed. When this happens in childhood, it can lead to long-term health and educational

problems. We may not like the fact that we are wired such that our well-being depends on our connection with others, but the facts are the facts.[58]

Many of us have had the dismal experience of walking past a clique in high school or even the office cafeteria, worrying that the "popular kids" are laughing at us. We certainly don't want others to see how insecure we are. And how do we react when a boss criticizes us in front of the whole team? If we were being authentic, we'd fall apart. But usually we put on a brave face and present another persona, one who's unaffected by a public lashing.

When we can put ourselves in the shoes of those who are hurting or angry and truly try to understand them and connect with them, that is when empathy occurs. We see them through new eyes and see how much we have in common with them. Alan Alda said, "The more empathy I have, the less annoying other people are."[59] That's funny but also very perceptive. When we show empathy, that is when we stop judging and start caring, which is the *sine qua non* of civility.

> *The most beautiful people we have known are those who have known defeat, known suffering, known struggle, known loss, and have found their way out of the depths. These persons have an appreciation, a sensitivity, and an understanding of life that fills them with compassion, gentleness, and a deep loving concern. Beautiful people do not just happen.*
>
> —*Elisabeth Kübler-Ross*

CHAPTER SEVEN

Trust

*Speak not injurious words neither in jest nor earnest.
Scoff at none although they give occasion.*

—Rule 65

*Be not apt to relate news if you know not the truth
thereof. In discoursing of things you have heard, name
not your author. Always a secret discover not.*

—Rule 79

*Undertake not what you cannot perform
but be careful to keep your promise.*

—Rule 82

Speak not evil of the absent, for it is unjust.

—Rule 89

You could say the above rules boil down to this: Hold back harmful words. Keep secrets, honor promises, and don't talk behind people's backs. These rules are not just about trusting others, but also about *earning* the trust of others.

Can you imagine how much better off we'd be if we all adhered to these time-tested rules? Maybe we could make genuine progress on those sticky workplace issues everyone avoids. Perhaps kids wouldn't be so anxious about how to make and keep friends. Even the best marriages might improve. Maybe Congress would be able to get past infighting and actually legislate—*together*.

We could also pretty quickly determine who in our own lives is trustworthy. Too often we're not sure—and that's stressful and isolating. When we don't trust those around us, we understandably feel the need to create a protective bubble around ourselves. Self-protection is just instinctive.

But shielding ourselves from difficult interactions ultimately comes at a long-term personal, social, and societal cost. Sure, we survive, but while we're fending off people whom we don't feel we can trust, we can't become our best selves. Why? Because to flourish, we need to take a risk in order to form bonds with other humans.

Trust is created through our relationships we can rely upon. The finest creations and our greatest moments are born in the crucible of human interaction where we feel unified, where all parties trust one another. We feel a sense of unity and belonging. Perhaps there is magic to be found in those moments precisely because they are rare.

In the time of COVID-19, the Black Lives Matter movement, the efforts to defund the police, and a particularly divisive political cycle, trust feels like it's at an all-time low. This is all the more reason for us to look inward to ponder what we can do to build trust in and among our neighborhoods and institutions.

Whom and What Can We Trust?

You'd think it would go without saying that everyone should tell the truth. But have you noticed that the definition of "truth" is getting harder to pin down? Every day, competing television networks and digital and paper media seem to give us different versions of the truth. Whose version, and what information, can we trust?

Sadly, many have given up on the concept of an objective news source. Each media outlet seems determined to push its own perspective on current events, which is fine if we're talking about an opinion piece. But the spin is now obliterating viewpoint-neutral journalism. Consequently, we're dealing with a confusing kaleidoscope of perspectives on what "truth" is.

Some try to manipulate or ignore facts in order to make them fit their agendas or align with their biases. Do we do that to ourselves as well? Fyodor Dostoevsky wrote, "A man who lies to himself and listens to his own lie comes to a point where he does not discern any truth either in himself or anywhere around him, and thus falls into disrespect towards himself and others."[60] Can we trust ourselves to see events and issues objectively?

Some people might say there are universal truths we can all agree on. The irony is, not everyone will agree with even *that*! Plenty of people don't believe universal truths exist. "Everything is relative," some say, since we each have our own highly individual and subjective perspective. We often mistake our opinion for "the truth."

But we can start with the facts, right? Or . . . can we?

During a criminal trial, a prosecutor and a defense attorney each have the job of laying out the facts to the jury. But those attorneys will *interpret* those facts in vastly different ways. In life, as in a courtroom, who's to say all the facts are on the table? Perhaps a defendant legitimately forgets some details of what happened. Other times, we intentionally don't share facts that could make us look bad or hurt someone we love. When this practice is a part of official legal proceedings, then how do we apply truth to our pledge to be civil and create more civility in the world? After all, truth and honesty *can* hurt people—or at least cause deeply hurt feelings. Is there a need to tell something true but unkind? We often mistake our opinion for "the truth."

Following the example of George Washington, whose restrained approach to personal interactions grew from his aversion to making people uncomfortable, I believe it's not always necessary to offer one's opinion in the name of "telling the truth" if that truth will hurt someone without a purpose of the greater good. Parents around the world counsel their children to consider three questions before they speak: "Is it true? Is it kind? Is it necessary?" If we cannot say yes to all three questions, should we say anything at all?

Trust can flourish with kindness, but kindness alone does not mean someone is trustworthy. Why are life and humanity and our interactions within it all so complicated? We are complex beings. We all have a unique existence on this planet; not one person's life is exactly the same as another's. Siblings do not have the same life just because they grew up in the same family. Friends do not have the same experiences or outlook just because they went to the same school.

Trust Is a Two-Way Street

Without trust, life can feel like a long and lonely road. We deplete lots of energy keeping our guard up just to preserve what's "ours" to protect. But humans need connection to other humans. With genuine two-way trust, not only can we survive, but we also can *thrive.*

We might innately understand that trust needs to go both ways for a productive, healthy, civil relationship. Even so, we tend to ignore our own role in creating and maintaining that trust. Shouldn't we ponder if *we* are worthy of trust? Most of us are confident we are, and we focus on "that person over there" and whether *they* fall short in the trust dynamic.

We're trustworthy. *We're* nice, and we mean well. How could anyone think otherwise? Just imagine someone doubting our good intentions! Haven't we felt our blood pressure rise just a little at the slightest insinuation that we can't be trusted?

The adrenaline starts to flow, and we're tempted to defend ourselves. *Sure, I mess up every once in a while,* we might think, *but I am a good person! How dare you think otherwise!* Spending time considering our own trustworthiness is uncomfortable, so we often don't explore it in depth.

Most people are decent and hold beliefs that mirror societal norms. They will approach life from different perspectives and experiences from yours or mine. Yes, there are exceptions, but almost every one of us harbors goodwill to our fellow humans. Most of us have a heart and genuinely want to encourage and support others. If our answer to the last statement is "not really," then we need to reexamine our own perspective and our own contribution to the world of trust. When we make the effort to lift up everyone, not just ourselves, we're ready to develop trust with the people in our lives—whether it's trust we give or trust we earn.

Trust is a foundational pillar in the concept of civility. When we open ourselves up to someone, even a little bit, we're in effect saying, "I trust you with this vulnerable part of me because in some way, shape, or form, this facet of me is in *you* too. Maybe we express it differently, but it's there. We are humans, all together." If only we could just say that! Sometimes it's hard to convey that we want to be friends or at the very least work or coexist together without drama or trauma or watching our backs all the time.

You and I can work together, even if our philosophies are radically different. We can agree to disagree, and we can decide together that we're not going to argue about certain issues. We can still establish trust even if we're in different political parties, different religions, or just rival schools. We actually can build up trust if we disagree with someone and say so. Disagreement does not negate trust; *dishonesty* negates trust.

This is the junction where we usually pair the words *trust* and *respect*. In this give-and-take, we must show respect for the viewpoints of others if others are to trust *us*. How does that work? When we disrespect another's opinion, we almost guarantee that our own opinions will not be given respect. Our perspective will be ignored, and people will be disinclined to trust our motives.

We might be watching out for our own professional interests or other weighty concerns—national security, a neighborhood legal matter, or a custody battle—that might preclude a close relationship. But to accomplish anything that benefits society requires a level of willingness on both sides to build trust and cooperate.

Ronald Reagan and Mikhail Gorbachev exhibited that kind of motivation to build trust between their countries—and they had to trust their teams to have that same kind of will and reliability. In the mid-1980s, the country was at a crucial turning point in our relationship with the Soviet Union. Reagan's interactions with Mikhail Gorbachev, the eighth and last leader of the Soviet Union, were textbook lessons on how to build and earn trust with adversaries.

At that time, the USSR was the greatest threat to the national security of the United States. Many people thought Reagan was "poking the bear" when he initiated the conversation with a Soviet leader. History has shown that he proved the naysayers wrong!

In November 1985, the two leaders held their first summit in Geneva, Switzerland. My peers Andrew Littlefair, Bob Schmidt, Joanne Drake, and others were in Geneva, working every detail of that event. I was part of the team holding down the fort at the White House. Given the significance of the summit, it's remarkable how much trust was placed in our little band of advance people* to plan and execute such a critical meeting.

Our crew was very young, but we were led by a couple of seasoned veterans, Jim Hooley and Bill Henkel, who in turn answered to Michael K. Deaver. We were trained and supervised by the very best, and they managed the overall plan in substance and logistics, but our young advance people carried a lot of weight on their shoulders as they negotiated with their Soviet counterparts on every microscopic detail of the visit. They had to build trust between the U.S. and Soviet teams quickly—if not complete trust, then at least mutual respect. While it was unlikely that a poor relationship with an advance person would derail world peace, our office certainly was charged with making sure that we built trust as part of our daily efforts representing President Reagan wherever we went.

The next year, when we were preparing the details for the president's trip to Moscow, our team went to a Russian *dacha* (country

---

* The Office of Presidential Advance executes all the details of every move the president of the United States makes outside the White House. We literally went "in advance" of the president to arrange the details of his trips. We worked closely with the USSS (Secret Service), the military office, the press office, the speechwriters, the travel office, the office of the chief of staff, and others to make sure all the plans were buttoned up.

house) to meet with our Soviet counterparts. The Soviet chief of protocol sat across a large table from our team that included Rick Ahearn (lead advance), Tom Pernice, Scott Lane, and me. Rick negotiated moving a microphone a few feet in the Kremlin and hundreds of other such details. I'll never forget the response from the Soviet chief of protocol on so many issues: "It's no problem; it's impossible!" We all still laugh about that to this day, and we recognize that the good humor was only possible because both sides trusted each other.

The Power of Character to Establish Trust

George Washington faced a daunting challenge when the thirteen colonies were rising to rebellion: he needed to inspire his fellow Americans to trust that he was the man to lead them. Many people still felt loyal to the king of England and were hesitant to join the revolution. The colonists needed a leader who could reach across a broad spectrum of people and interests and bring them together.

What did he do to inspire them?

He did not attempt to impress them with his intelligence. Washington never went to college, and he knew that men far more learned than he were in his company. Historian Edmund Morgan wrote that Washington "had none of the range of the brilliant men around, the intellectual curiosity of a Jefferson, the fiscal genius of a Hamilton."[61] However, Morgan continued, "in his understanding of power he left them all behind."[62] Washington understood that the key to power and leadership is trust, and he knew better than any how to foster trust among the citizenry. His deep-rooted comprehension of his fellow Americans was an essential catalyst for moving the country forward.

Surely the colonists could only have relied on a man with a solid character and impeccable integrity. They would only have had confidence in a man who adhered to a strict code of conduct. Only a man with these qualities could have inspired the colonists to trust him, join the rebellion, and support his strategy.

While other political leaders might have stirred the pot and intimidated or bullied the states into getting it together—so much was at stake, and tempers were high—General Washington remained focused on his goal of unity. He was a great admirer of stoicism, the endurance of hardship without complaint. He was a man of great restraint and self-discipline. He employed quiet but firm strategies that inspired trust in him as a leader. America owes him a great debt for his remarkable character and forbearance. Because the colonists trusted him, he was able to keep them united and form a new nation.

The Building Blocks: Patience and Steadiness

Those who seek to build trust at any level wrestle with the same concern George Washington did: How do we cultivate real trust among and between members of our personal and professional communities? A good start is to emulate Washington's conscious efforts to remain patient, steady, and calm. An even temper did not come easily to him—he had to work on it. Thomas Jefferson once said of our first president, "His temper was naturally irritable and high-toned; but reflection & resolution had obtained a firm and habitual ascendency over it."[63]

Here's an example of how a patient, steady nature builds trust. Moire, my best friend since seventh grade, is a lifelong lover of all things "horse." An accomplished horsewoman, she's been riding since she was about five years old. We bonded quickly while riding, although she far surpassed my skills in the equine arena. Recently, we had a chat about her new horse, Max, and how she is struggling to connect with him while carriage driving. In effect, she's working to build a trust-based relationship with this spirited thoroughbred. He's a good horse and is stunningly beautiful. The problem is they don't trust one another—yet. Is Moire worthy of trust? Of course! But the horse doesn't know that, so she must earn his trust. He has trust issues, but so does she. They both come to the arena with a little baggage.

Moire had a couple of frightening experiences while driving another horse, so she's cautious when a horse is not quite "with the program." That's certainly understandable, but we know a horse can sense the insecurities and hesitance of the rider. Unfortunately, Max does not know Moire's story. Similarly, Max can't verbally communicate his own issues to Moire, who only senses the horse's reluctance. By controlling her emotions, exhibiting patience, presenting an even-tempered nature, and trusting in herself (and in a trainer who has an unbiased perspective), Moire knows she can help her new horse to trust her. It's working, but it takes time.

My friend's challenge is to just be patient and kind with the horse and herself until Max feels comfortable and safe enough to trust her. Yes, there is technique and training involved, but she can help him overcome his emotional issues, and they can move forward together. She also knows she must trust herself and her own abilities to bring this horse along with her. It takes consistency, and over time they are building that bridge of trust between them.

Some years ago, I had a simple learning experience about building trust. For almost twenty-eight years, I lived on the other side of the country from my parents. In December 2012, I went home to California to celebrate my dad's seventy-fourth birthday and Christmas. It quickly became apparent that my parents were struggling. They were dealing with complex business and economy issues as well as age-related health challenges that made the business concerns seem all the more overwhelming.

One morning, my father confided in me. "I could use some help with a few things I'm dealing with," he admitted. The lump in my throat made it hard to swallow. My father had never asked me for help before. Until that day, *he* had always been the one to give the help to his three daughters. In that moment, my path was clear, and I told him I would stay and help them with whatever they needed until they didn't need my help anymore.

My sisters pitched in, of course; everyone had their part in helping our family overcome a painful and stressful time. I was grateful that I was at a stage in my life where I could offer my parents "the gift of my presence" to support them. I had the ability to physically be there for them.

So, in the middle of my life, I moved home, into my sister Kelly's old high school bedroom directly underneath the master bedroom. From my perspective, it was a pretty easy transition. I enjoy change and like a challenge. But for my parents, I'm sure it was more than a little disruptive to their long-established routines—even though I knew they were delighted to have me home, along with the extra pair of hands. At first, they would ask if I'd remembered to turn off the stove, put down the garage door, turn off the porch light, or lock the front door. I would reassure them that I had indeed done all these things—at least most of the time!

I knew they weren't trying to be difficult or implying they couldn't trust me. I understood and knew they believed in me. We just needed to get used to living together again. We needed time to develop the faith that each of us would take care of our responsibilities to each other and to the home that, for now, I was sharing with them. Living in a home together is like being on a team: everyone has their role.

Gradually, my parents stopped asking if I'd followed through—not because they cared any less, but because they could see, over and over, through the small acts incorporated into our days together, that I was an earnest, reliable teammate and helper. Despite tough times on the health and business front, it was—and remains—a very special time together.

Through this experience, I relearned what built trust: I didn't rush to judgment with my parents, and I gave them the benefit of the doubt that they were not trying to control me or be critical. I was patient. I remained calm and even-tempered. Their questions didn't offend me, even though they might have sounded like they didn't trust me. Through repeated and consistent behavior on my part, I believe I was able to show them I was up to the task of the daily work our cohabitation required, which built mutual trust.

Does my dad still ask if I have gas in my car or the bridge toll gizmo or if I made sure to not let the cat out after dark? Yes, he does, and I love it. That's also the way he shows he cares. President Reagan's famous words about working with the Soviets may apply here: "Trust, but verify."[64]

Trust doesn't happen overnight. It takes time and genuine effort by both parties to demonstrate their interest in creating a strong bond affixed by reliance and confidence. Trust comes through small, mindful actions that build upon one another. Bit by bit, these small, repetitive acts demonstrate our ability to be trusted. And trust allows us to build connections.

The Gentle Influence of Humor and Informality

There's nothing like using humor to release tension or build trust. Reagan and Gorbachev both knew the value of employing humor to prop up and even extend moments of mutual understanding.

How can we maintain an opposing party's or even just our parents' trust in us? For a start, we can find something both parties can laugh about. Yes, it's risky—they might not think we're funny—but nothing worthwhile comes easily or without risk. The reward, in this case, was that the world changed for the better. What if our attempt falls flat? We can try anyway. We might not achieve world peace, but if we can make our own corner of the globe a little friendlier, we can still make an important difference.

Another seemingly small gesture that engenders trust is creating an atmosphere of comfort and easy familiarity. When Reagan and Gorbachev called each other by their first names at the signing of the INF treaty, the event made international news.

> An immediate mood of warmth was established as the two leaders agreed this morning to call each other by their first names, a White House official said. He quoted the President as telling Mr. Gorbachev, "My first name is Ron."
> Mr. Gorbachev answered, "Mine is Mikhail."
> "When we're working in private session," Mr. Reagan reportedly said, "we can call each other that."[65]

Something as simple as calling someone by their first name helps build a connection. When we're willing to participate in this level of informality, it can be a sign of emerging trust. What if we introduced ourselves by our first names at our next business meeting with someone whose trust we want to earn? Even if formality is the cultural norm, it wouldn't hurt to try. If the other person offers their first name, too, we're on our way to establishing trust. Just a first step, easy to take. The responsibility to build a lasting trust is ours from that point forward. And it's our behavior that will be the final determinant.

Reagan and Gorbachev—the champion of freedom and the leader of the evil empire—became true friends. It's important to remember that Gorbachev himself was not evil. He was just a man leading a Communist country that Reagan, in 1983, had dubbed "the evil empire" because of its lack of human rights and individual freedoms. Certainly, evil leaders like Stalin in the past had committed atrocious crimes against humanity. But by the early 1980s, Gorbachev was leading a country that was dying under its own weight.

President Reagan gave this man a chance to reach across the table and do something good for the world: mutual nuclear disarmament. Gorbachev reached back. Sadly, and I suppose understandably, Gorbachev is not regaled as a hero in Russia. From the perspective of believers in freedom, however, General Secretary Gorbachev was a courageous man who had everything to lose—and did.

Throughout these stories, the key concept that stitches them together is *rapport*. Politicians and everyday people who develop and maintain rapport find a space for trust and build a relationship that can weather challenges.

Listen without Compromising Values

Some of these challenges might be different opinions and philosophies.

Can we trust someone who doesn't share our values? Can they trust us? Those values may be very different from our own. How do we abide by our principles yet remain civil while talking to someone whose values don't align with ours?

While we should be able to share what's important to us, pushing our views on others may not be the best way to build rapport either. I try to express my values through the organizations I support, the company I keep, and the work I do—in other words, through actions. I have ample opportunity to assert my principles as I unwrap this wondrous gift called life. I know I am fortunate to live in a free country, where I have the right to pursue my dreams and express myself freely. But just because I *can* express myself freely doesn't mean I *should*.

Not everyone is as fortunate—I try to remember that even as I try to stand by my principles. Because I am so grateful for the ability to take a position on whatever subject I choose to address, I am all the more willing to listen to the values of friends, colleagues, and ideological adversaries. Perhaps they don't get a chance to state their opinions very often; perhaps they lack a caring and understanding support system. Can I show grace and be a sympathetic ear?

Listening to and building trust with someone from, say, a different religion or different political party does not require compromising our values. Do both parties have to meet in the middle? President Reagan showed that we don't need to concede our values to cooperate with those who don't share them.

In the summer of 1988, Reagan and Gorbachev again had a

summit meeting, this time in Moscow. I was part of the advance team, and witnessing this historic visit was one of the most exciting moments of my life, personally and professionally.

Reagan's goal at the Moscow Summit was to find even more common ground with the USSR and thus strengthen their trust. The whole world watched in awe as President Reagan, a devout anti-Communist, walked through Red Square with Gorbachev, a committed Marxist. When a reporter asked President Reagan about his "evil empire" speech in 1983, he responded, "I was talking about another time, another era."[66] Gorbachev and his fellow countrymen appreciated the conciliatory words.

But despite his desire for peace and trust between the two countries, our president would not compromise American values to achieve it. A reporter noted that "at every opportunity, Ronald Reagan preached the virtues of entrepreneurship, freedom of expression, and limited government."[67] And he would not agree on further arms limitations talks with the Soviet leader; he didn't feel it was in America's best interest to do so. Reagan was eager to establish a relationship with the USSR, but he wanted proof that the Soviets were keeping their promises. ("Trust, but verify.") In the end, it was a productive summit, a goodwill event that connected the two leaders even more.

When we negotiate with an opposing party or simply want to bridge the gap with someone we don't entirely trust, it's possible to do so without sacrificing our core values. Like President Reagan, we can present who we are with confidence. At the same time, we can look for ways to show that we want to earn trust. We can interject sincere warmth and optimism—trademarks of the Reagan approach—into the conversation. Don't be afraid to reach out and put a spotlight on something positive the other person is doing. Say so out loud.

The powerful effect of genuinely speaking well of and cheering on someone else's efforts or accomplishments can work wonders on a developing relationship of trust.

I recently chatted with longtime friend Bob Dold, a former congressman from Illinois known for his ability to work across the aisle. I asked about his time on Capitol Hill and how he managed to create cordial relationships and even close friendships with other members of Congress who held different beliefs and political philosophies. What he said really struck me, "It's terribly hard to hate up close."

Lower the Walls between Foes

President Reagan was known as "the Great Communicator," and he had good rapport with many Democrats in Congress. Nevertheless, he endured significant criticism from liberals in Congress and a veritable hailstorm of negativity in the press throughout his eight years in office. It wasn't until after his presidency ended that his critics began to recognize Reagan's exceptional leadership skills and his ongoing bipartisan efforts to develop trust and unify the country. He had a way of speaking to our hearts that reminded Americans what we all have in common: a desire for peace, prosperity, and freedom.

Democratic members of Congress encouraged other Republicans to follow in Reagan's footsteps and seek out win-wins. They especially admired how President Reagan was able to form a working friendship with Democrat House Speaker Thomas P. "Tip" O'Neill. They might have been on opposing sides of many issues, but after 6:00 p.m. on quite a few workdays, they would sit down for drinks at the White House. Despite their considerable differences, they were just two Americans fighting for their country's well-being.

Giving someone a glimpse into our personal side—the way

Reagan and Tip O'Neill did when they had a drink together—is key to lowering the walls between foes and setting up mutually beneficial results. Until we recognize our own weaknesses and fallibility, we won't be willing to engage in give-and-take and reach solutions to our mutual problems. And when we're frustrated by a lack of progress, we can use President Reagan's example as an unflagging optimist to inspire us to go for a win-win.

He sincerely wanted every citizen to benefit in some way. Former president Barack Obama described Reagan as appealing to a uniquely American sentiment: "We want clarity, we want optimism, we want a return to that sense of dynamism and entrepreneurship that had been missing."[68] That's why so many people trusted him—and why he's the epitome of civility.

CHAPTER EIGHT

Respect and Honor

Wherein you reprove another, be unblameable yourself, for example is more prevalent than precepts.

—Rule 48

Never express anything unbecoming, nor act against the rules of moral[ity] . . .

—Rule 59

When you speak of God or His attributes, let it be seriously and with reverence.

Honor and obey your natural parents although they be poor.

—Rule 108

One of our most human of traits is having a conscience, the inner voice that identifies right from wrong. Another way to look at this is through the prism of the concept of *honor*, defined as "a fine sense of and strict allegiance to what is due or right" and "as a moral bounden duty: sometimes implying that there is no legal obligation."[69] Acting with honor is essential to the practice of civility, and George Washington is a definitive example.

Young George was only eleven years old when his father died. His mother, Mary Ball Washington, was "an exceptionally strong and resilient woman, a single mother who raised five children and instilled in them qualities of fortitude and purpose."[70] George and his younger siblings helped her run the family farm instead of going to boarding school in England, as was the custom among Virginia landowners. As he worked long hours on the farm, the future president learned that hardy resolve mixed with courage went a long way to providing a sense of satisfaction and purpose in life.

A strict, religious mother, Mary expected absolute obedience from her children. Her example as a resolute matriarch no doubt helped forge George's strong character and his ability to surmount huge challenges, just as his mother had. Above all, Mary's absolute convictions of what was right and wrong honed his sense of honor: "In letters he sent his mother throughout his adolescence, George often addressed her as 'Honoured Madam,' which some interpret as a lack of affection. Rather, it speaks to the respect and courtesy she instilled in him."[71]

Is "Honor" Subjective?

The various definitions of honor lead, in some extreme cases, to horrifying results. Nearly thirty documented duels—or "affairs of honor," as they were once called—have occurred throughout the history of the United States, and many more have taken place worldwide. Perhaps the most famous and currently revisited American duel took place in 1804. Alexander Hamilton, one of our nation's Founding Fathers, detested Thomas Jefferson's vice president, Aaron Burr. When Burr ran for governor of New York, Hamilton attacked Burr's character and passionately campaigned against him. Burr lost the race and challenged Hamilton to a duel to restore his reputation and honor. In the gunfight, he shot Hamilton, who died of his injuries a few days later.[72]

Unfortunately, defending family honor is not a relic of a bygone era. So-called "honor" killings—the vicious murder of women, girls, and homosexuals who "bring shame" to their family name—still happen all too often throughout the world. According to long-standing cultural tradition, a family is justified in killing the person who caused the "dishonor." The offenses run a wide gamut: simply talking to a member of the opposite sex, dressing inappropriately, refusing to marry a selected suitor, or eloping with someone not chosen by the family. Having sexual relations outside of marriage is high on the list of justifications for "honor" killing.

Those are extreme examples of how the concept of honor can be twisted—fortunately, most rational human beings share roughly the same objective definition of right and wrong, the standard of integrity, and the value of character. The ideal of honor has given rise to some of the most awe-inspiring moments in history.

In 2019 I had the privilege of interviewing Lieutenant Commander Robert H. Shumaker (U.S. Navy, ret.), who talked to me about his experiences as a prisoner of war in the "Hanoi Hilton" during the Vietnam War, alongside the late senator John McCain. Despite repeated torture for years, LCDR Shumaker would only give his name, rank, serial number, and date of birth to his captors. Finally, the North Vietnamese soldiers tortured him to such an unimaginable extent that he revealed the name of his hometown. Shumaker agonized about what he thought had brought dishonor to his country, but the opposite was true.

As a way to pass the time (when he was not being tortured), Shumaker built the house of his dreams in his mind brick by brick. When he was done, he took it apart and rebuilt it again until it was perfected.

Meanwhile, in another display of honor and devotion, Lorraine Shumaker waited for her husband all those years while he was imprisoned, and she never gave up hope.

After eight horrific years of imprisonment, he returned home to an exceptionally grateful family and country and built that house and lives in it with his wife. His behavior while in prison was—and continues to be—the highest form of honor; "We stayed loyal to our beliefs, and true to our country," he said in an interview.[73]

ACTING WITH HONOR OFTEN REQUIRES SACRIFICE

The Smithsonian's National Museum of American History Kenneth E. Behring Center is named for the late Ken Behring. Ken was a friend and hired me to help him in 2004 with the opening of the museum's exhibit "The Price of Freedom: Americans at War." While dealing with the usual issues of protocol, logistics, invitation lists, and so forth, I had time to wander through the exhibit prior to its opening to the public. I think it's the first time I had ever thought about the "price" of freedom. Now, I always think of honoring all service members who gave their lives so we could have freedom of expression, freedom of movement, freedom to protest, and freedom to live where we like, to travel, and to just live in peace. Those who paid the ultimate price for defending our values and our way of life always deserve our honor and respect.

My father introduced me to General MacArthur's famous speech at West Point. Even now I can hear that gravelly voice emanating from a crackling recording of that speech:

> I do not know the dignity of their birth, but I do know the glory of their death. They died unquestioning, uncomplaining, with faith in their hearts, and on their lips the hope that we would go on to victory. Always for them: Duty, Honor, Country.[74]

All of us, at some point in our lives, face the unenviable position of having to choose between honor—and all the struggle, fear, and sacrifice it entails—and doing something easier. Perhaps we ask ourselves, *Who will know if we don't choose the path of honor?* And if we think no one will find out, we might consider abandoning our principles.

Whenever I'm tempted to detour around the honorable choice, I think of the paradoxical commandments that Mother Teresa pasted on the wall of her children's home in Calcutta. Part of it includes these brave, inspiring words:

> The good you do will be forgotten tomorrow.
> Do good anyway.
> Give the world the best you have
> And you'll get kicked in the teeth.
> Give the world the best you've got anyway.[75]

Doing the right thing is really between our Higher Power and us. We sleep better every time we choose the harder road that leads to honor. Of course, it's difficult, because it requires the very best effort we have to offer the world: integrity, love, and courage. Too often we don't believe we have what it takes, but we do.

Can you think of a time in your life when you chose honor over ease? Were you scared? Most of us are. But if we are honorable, we do it anyway.

Respect Is Honor in Action

> *Every action done in company ought to be with some sign of respect to those that are present.*
>
> *–Rule 1*

Honor is both a noun and a verb, and its verb form is often listed as a synonym of *respect*. In fact, you could say respect is honor in action. "To honor" means to "pay worthy respect to (by some outward action)" and "to celebrate."[76] In the sixteenth century, bending the knee in a curtsy (a variation of the word *courtesy*) was a customary expression of respect.

Over and over, George Washington honored his troops by showing his respect for the militia through his actions. Part of his growth as a military leader came from listening to his generals' advice and observing the emotions of and comments from his foot soldiers. During that legendary snowy winter at Valley Forge, where all were physically and mentally exhausted, Washington made the same sacrifices he asked of his men. His often-formal behavior belied his compassion and thoughtfulness. He walked or rode alone among his soldiers, inquiring after their welfare. He showed them on a daily basis that he believed they would succeed, and he did not esteem himself any higher than the soldiers who were fighting for independence. In modern parlance, he didn't just talk the talk; George Washington walked the walk.

After he was elected president, Washington made two epic journeys to visit his fellow citizens: one through the northern states, and the other an arduous nineteen-hundred-mile trek to the south. These trips were physically taxing; a man of sixty as he was would have found the rough roads and carriage rides strenuous. By honoring his compatriots with his sacrificial trek, President Washington demonstrated the value he placed on his men. Through his actions, he signaled that inside each of them was the potential for greatness. His actions showed the soldiers that they were worthy of his effort.

These are but a few examples that show how much our first president esteemed and appreciated the new Americans, how much he celebrated their lives and accomplishments. He showed respect to others, and that is why he garnered respect wherever he went and maintains it through the ages.

Profoundly gratified and inspired by Washington's honorable character and devotion to their cause, his army and countrymen passed on their deep respect for him to their children, their grandchildren, and beyond. To this day, we honor and celebrate George Washington as one of the greatest Americans who ever lived. That admiration and esteem expands as we plow through complicated times that require our first president's degree of unyielding commitment to our founding principles.

Let Others Know We See Them

"R-E-S-P-E-C-T." We all know the Otis Redding song, later made more famous by Aretha Franklin. Aside from how catchy the tune is, one reason it's remained such an iconic anthem is because Franklin sang it when minority rights were on the front burner for the first time since the Civil War. At the same time, women were demanding equal rights, and the country was ready to have a conversation about human dignity and our obligation to protect it—which we do through showing respect and behaving respectfully.

As a protocol officer at the U.S. Department of State, and later in my own business, I built an entire career around the concept of respect. I worked to support the dignity of other people. I opened doors instead of closing them—both metaphorically and literally. (The simple act of opening a door for someone conveys the message that we put others first.)

One of my first clients in my business, Practical Protocol, was the president of Poland, Lech Walesa. His storied history and trajectory from shipyard worker to dissident to Nobel Peace Prize recipient to first democratically elected president of Poland is something to behold. To be honest, I was a little nervous talking to him.

We were on a ferry we had hired to take the president and his delegation to Ellis Island. While we cruised, I knelt beside him to explain, through the interpreter, what would happen once we arrived on Ellis Island. After a few minutes, President Walesa tapped me on the shoulder and pointed his two fingers at my eyes and then his—the universal signal to look someone in the eyes. Although I had been talking to the president, I had been looking at the interpreter. President Walesa said, "My interpreter will tell me what you are saying, but you are speaking to *me*."

He was right. In my nervous state, I thought I was being respectful by not looking at him, but it was really the opposite. I appreciate the respect he showed me by signaling that what I had to say was important to him.

When we got off the ferry at Ellis Island, we took a picture together. Lech Walesa was on one side of me, and his wife was on the other. As the photographer said "smile," the president of Poland goosed me—he pinched my side a little to make me smile. Today, some might take offense at an action like that, but I knew he was trying to break the ice and make me feel more comfortable with him. We were able to be less formal from that point forward, but we still treated each other with dignity and respect.

Everyone, no matter their age or position in society, desires respect. Take our parents and grandparents. They might not beat us at arm wrestling anymore, and many can't easily hear our stories due to failing ears—or perhaps they have a hard time even remembering their own. Regardless, they don't want to be marginalized or ignored. They want younger people to acknowledge their years of experience and to honor them. We can show respect by helping them maintain their dignity, despite the lack of full physical and sometimes slowing capacities.

Leslie Lautenslager, executive assistant to Gen. Colin Powell (U.S. Army, ret.), is serving a term as president of PDI-POA (Protocol and Diplomacy International–Protocol Officers Association), my industry's trade organization. For the annual conference in San Diego, California, Leslie invited me to keynote a presentation on civility. I arrived for the pre-speech luncheon to find I had been seated next to Leslie. It was blistering hot, and being the protocol professionals we all are, we were dressed in suits. Leslie and I were seated in the shade, but we were next to an older gentleman who was sitting in the sun. We twice offered him our seats, because we were concerned for his well-being, but he politely refused.

I could tell Leslie's brain was whirring—she was not going to give up. After some strategic patience, she leaned over to the gentleman and said, "You know, I have been indoors all day long, and I would love a chance to get some vitamin D. Would you mind changing places with me so I can sit in the sun a little?" He was happy to oblige. Leslie showed him respect and preserved his dignity, and all it took was some clever thoughtfulness.

CHAPTER NINE

My Practice of Civility

I personally pledge to contribute to a perpetual practice of civility.

My goal is to form a more perfect union, a more perfect world, and more perfect relationships, one civil act at a time. I am hopeful that through my own behavior of treating people well, my fellow man will reciprocate.

I acknowledge I am but a small and temporary part of the human race. With the remainder of my time, I will constantly strive to live up to my responsibilities to humanity through self-awareness and look to humility to self-correct when I stray from that course.

> *If you carry joy in your heart, you can heal any moment.*
> —*Carlos Santana*

I will be forgiving to my fellow man—not because I am so enlightened as to pity him, but because I have an open heart and understand that I am just as flawed and imperfect as the next person.

I can do my part to work toward justice for all by being civil to all.*

- **Courtesy.** I endeavor always to practice the Golden Rule and treat others as or better than I would hope to be treated.

- **Humility.** I hope one day to fully comprehend true humility as I strive for a life of purpose and meaning, with the contradiction of knowing I am both nothing and I am everything all at once. In this way I will come to know my true worth, my true responsibility, and my true place in this life, and I will begin to make a difference.

- **Empathy.** I pledge to be a lifelong learner, continuously improving my ability to understand other points of view, and seek common ground.

- **Trust.** I work to build trust through my words and deeds.

- **Respect and Honor.** I strive to live an honorable life and to honor others by showing respect.

I choose a life of joy and civility. I resolve to find joy in something every day. Instead of just being grateful, I promise to tell my family, friends, and many others how grateful I am for their presence in my life.

I promise to consider those who confound me to be my greatest teachers.

I believe we are responsible for our own happiness and behaviors and will not blame others if something is not right in my

---

* As we discussed in chapter 4, there are times in the civilized world when civility and personal safety conflict. When faced with physical harm, we must look to our instinctive fight-or-flight response to understand danger and react accordingly, ever hopeful that violence does not prevail.

life. It is my choice how I react to hardship, sadness, and distress. I am not a victim.

Rather than being tangled up in rules of civility, we can know that it is in our character and in our hearts where civility rules.

CONCLUSION

July 4, 2020

Dear America:

It's the 244th birthday of the United States of America as I bring this exercise of exploring civility to a close and prepare to hand it over to ForbesBooks to put it out there in the world. It's a little nerve-racking, to tell you the truth. I have been working on putting my thoughts to paper for almost seven years.

One would think in that time I could have written *War and Peace*! Maybe in some ways (I say humbly and ironically), I did. Completion of this book seemed to become such a moving target. Just as I was ready to conclude it, the landscape looked so different that I needed to reevaluate the proposition wearing a new lens. In those seven short years, so much has changed.

My own life and work focus changed by moving from Washington, D.C., back home to California to help my parents through health and business changes.

Then the tenor of the country shifted with the election of President Trump to the White House. Whether you love him or hate him, you can recognize that his presidency has changed all our interactions with one another—as friends, as family, as citizens.

Autonomous vehicles became a real prospect, and with that came the realization that humans may not actually be required for much in a future with artificial intelligence on the horizon. It's an interesting thought as I write about humanity—a challenge for us to get it together before the machines do.

The winter of 2020 brought COVID-19 to the world, threatening not only our way of life yet again, but our actual lives. As of this writing, it still affects our everyday activities and the ways in which we interact with our fellow humans, forcing a greater distance between us physically. We struggle to keep ourselves emotionally and mentally healthy in isolation and strive to find and new innovative ways to connect with one another.

By summer, pandemic-based unemployment, physical isolation, and loneliness connected with generations of pent-up angst, and inequalities that remain in our society all came together in a flammable combination to ignite the Black Lives Matter movement in a way that consumed the country.

Each moment in history is heavy with significance. But time is feather light, fleeting, and not to be wasted. *We* are in such a place in time that *We* the People can make a difference. *We* are fortunate to live in a society that still allows for freedom of expression, as messy as it may be. *We* cannot forget that, ever. As I expressed in the beginning of this journey, one voice does not a democracy make.

Ronald Reagan famously said:

> Freedom is a fragile thing and is never more than one generation away from extinction. It is not ours by inheritance; it must be fought for and defended constantly by each generation, for it comes only once to a people. Those who have known freedom and then lost it have never known it again.[77]

To achieve something, some choose protest; others choose violence using the Old Testament's justification of an "eye for an eye." I choose civility.

When I began my practice, I thought this was just a good way for me to live in peace and take a step toward personal fulfillment, purpose, and the pursuit of happiness. What I came to realize is that civility is an inherent component of democracy and that democracy is at stake *now*. The need for a practice of civility is critical to our future.

Now, I admit, throughout the significant societal shifts that have occurred and all the shifts still to come since I began this journey, I have questioned more than once whether I should even continue writing this book. Is civility obsolete? Is a pursuit of civility "feckless," as a friend of mine says in her Facebook posts? Should we just burn it all down instead as she suggests?

Who am I to talk about civility? Should I rewrite the whole book and omit George Washington because he owned slaves? Does owning slaves in a time more than 240 years ago when it was the common practice invalidate everything else? On the one hand, perhaps yes. On the other . . . perhaps we need to talk more about that.

After much contemplation, I decided that I can practice my own philosophy. This book is the way I look at life. Perhaps the concepts embedded in a practice of civility will resonate with you. Perhaps they will not. That's OK. That's the point, after all. We need to be able to talk to one another, whether we agree or not. It's not about silencing others or ourselves, but rather about trying to present our views in a way that can be heard. What's *not* OK is bullying or criticizing another person because their views differ from ours.

Human slavery is abhorrent to me. After everything I have written about civility and listening to others' views, ironically, I am not sure I could ever come to understand any rationalization that condones human bondage of any form. The fact is that human slavery exists and persists to this day and is hiding in plain sight. It's now, today, that we have any ability to do something to make change. It's now that I want to help be a part of the solution. Long ago I determined that a portion of the proceeds of this book would go to fight something that makes my skin crawl: human trafficking. We focus on the sins of the past, yet we do not talk about the slavery happening right under our noses.

Neil Armstrong's famous words as he stepped on the moon for the first time come to mind: "One small step for man, one giant leap for mankind." With each small step in a practice of civility, we can be freed from the weight of our own egos. We can embrace the fact that we humans are just one tiny part of something so much greater.

I love to quote a poem my dad wrote as a young man: "Mountains to climb, so little time." We have many mountains ahead of us. But the little secret is that there will always be another mountain to climb. Once we summit one, all we see is the vast, infinite range of mountains ahead. But with this practice of civility combined with taking the time to find joy in the small wonders of life, we can look around at the peak of each mountain we climb and take a moment to enjoy the journey, warts and all.

With humility at our core, we can actually, individually, do something remarkable and positive to contribute to the betterment of mankind. While we are free to be so, we are not our best selves in blame and anger and hate. We cannot be aspirational when hate weighs us down, when we burn down things we don't like, when we cannot talk with our neighbor about topics on which we disagree. I know I want to be a part of a positive, forward-moving mankind. I have come to believe that a practice of civility is a place to start to release ourselves from the shackles of anger and hate toward our fellow imperfect humans.

How can I say all this knowing that America was literally the child of revolution, that its short history has seen some of the most remarkable and important accomplishments mankind has seen yet is weighed down by its need to own some of the most destructive and despicable practices, like its role in human slavery?

The truth is, I don't know. In all my contemplation, I can only say I know that mankind is flawed, that I am flawed. I know that the tech world's start-up terminology comes to mind: "fail fast." When we fail—and we do, and we will—let's fail fast and iterate. Let's learn and grow from those mistakes.

But let's be thoughtful in the re-creation. Simply erasing, tearing down, or cutting off access to information we don't deem appropriate for our time is a mistake of such immense magnitude that our society might be permanently crippled and unable to reach its true potential. It might be destroyed in a way no one will want.

Humanity is complicated, and there are very real consequences for all the actions we take. Civility makes it possible to talk, discuss, debate, evolve, and make positive changes through its essential elements of courtesy to others; earning the trust of others; honoring and respecting our past, present, and future; and approaching our fellow humans with empathy and humility.

We can acknowledge our failings, make amends, and move on.

We can realize that love is more abundant and healing than hate for our society and ourselves. If we live in a constant state of rage and hate and blaming others, we only perpetuate problems. As individuals, we truly poison ourselves from the inside out. Again, I return to civility as fundamentally taking personal responsibility to be a part of the solution.

Yes, I am hopeful my many cherished friends around the globe outside the United States will find value in these pages, as I believe the concepts are applicable to all mankind. But I now know this book is my love letter to America.

I am thankful to be an American. The American Experiment is still and will always be a spectacular and unique work in progress. We are and will be always in a state of becoming a more perfect union.

I celebrate the brilliance of our founders who were flawed humans like you and me but also so wise to constitutionalize the inalienable rights of its people. And I am ever mindful of the responsibility I have to uphold my end of the bargain as a citizen.

> *Never doubt that a small group of thoughtful, committed citizens can change the world: indeed, it's the only thing that ever has.*
>
> —*Margaret Mead*

As I reflect on our nation's birthday while I bring this book to a close, I've concluded that we celebrate birthdays to remind us that we exist. We celebrate to remind ourselves that the first step to becoming new and improved is being here to take that step. We celebrate birth because there is so much hope and joy in the potential. Each successive birthday is a chance to renew our outlook and our behavior, to rise to the challenges of another year on earth. Individually we can work on our own journey to self-improvement. Collectively, we can grow more civil, even as we become more civilized.

In the musical *Hamilton*, composer Lin-Manuel Miranda wrote a song in which Hamilton says, "I'm not throwing away my shot." I know I won't, and I'm hopeful you won't either.

We will be our best selves, our best nation, our best world, when *civility rules!*

WASHINGTON'S RULES OF CIVILITY & DECENT BEHAVIOR IN COMPANY AND CONVERSATION

1. Every action done in company ought to be with some sign of respect to those that are present.

2. When in company, put not your hands to any part of the body not usually discovered.

3. Show nothing to your friend that may affright him.

4. In the presence of others, sing not to yourself with a humming noise, nor drum with your fingers or feet.

5. If you cough, sneeze, sigh, or yawn, do it not loud but privately; and speak not in your yawning, but put your handkerchief or hand before your face and turn aside.

6. Sleep not when others speak, sit not when others stand, speak not when you should hold your peace, walk not on when others stop.

7. Put not off your clothes in the presence of others, nor go out your chamber half dressed.

8. At play and at fire, it's good manners to give place to the last comer and affect not to speak louder than ordinary.

9. Spit not in the fire, nor stoop low before it, neither put your hands into the flames to warm them, nor set your feet upon the fire, especially if there be meat before it.

10. When you sit down, keep your feet firm and even, without putting one on the other or crossing them.

11. Shift not yourself in the sight of others, nor gnaw your nails.

12. Shake not the head, feet, or legs, roll not the eyes, lift not one eyebrow higher than the other, wry not the mouth, and bedew no man's face with your spittle by approaching too near him when you speak.

13. Kill no vermin as fleas, lice, ticks, etc., in the sight of others; if you see any filth or thick spittle, put your foot dexterously upon it. If it be upon the clothes of your companions, put it off privately, and if it be upon your own clothes, return thanks to him who puts it off.

14. Turn not your back to others, especially in speaking; jog not the table or desk on which another reads or writes; lean not upon anyone.

15. Keep your nails clean and short, also your hands and teeth clean, yet without showing any great concern for them.

16. Do not puff up the cheeks, loll not out the tongue, rub the hands or beard, thrust out the lips or bite them, or keep the lips too open or too close[d].

17. Be no flatterer, neither play with any that delights not to be played withal.

18. Read no letters, books, or papers in company, but when there is a necessity for the doing of it, you must ask leave. Come not near the books or writings of another so as to read them, unless desired, or give your opinion of them unasked. Also, look not nigh when another is writing a letter.

19. Let your countenance be pleasant, but in serious matters somewhat grave.

20. The gestures of the body must be suited to the discourse you are upon.

21. Reproach none for the infirmities of nature, nor delight to put them that have in mind thereof.

22. Show not yourself glad at the misfortune of another, though he were your enemy.

23. When you see a crime punished, you may be inwardly pleased; but always show pity to the suffering offender.

24. Do not laugh too loud or too much at any public spectacle.

25. Superfluous compliments and all affection of ceremony are to be avoided, yet where due they are not to be neglected.

26. In pulling off your hat to persons of distinctions, [such] as noblemen, justices, churchmen, etc., make a reverence, bowing more or less according to the custom of the better bred and quality of the persons. Amongst your equals, expect not always that they should begin with you first, but to pull off the hat when there is no need is affectation. In the manner of saluting and re-saluting in words, keep to the usual custom.

27. 'Tis ill manners to bid one more eminent than yourself be covered, as well as not to do it to whom it's due. Likewise, he that makes too much haste to put on his hat does not well, yet he ought to put it on at the first, or at most the second time of being asked. Now what is herein spoken of qualification in behavior in saluting ought also to be observed in taking of place, and sitting down for ceremonies without bounds is troublesome.

28. If anyone come to speak to you while you are sitting, stand up though he be your inferior, and when you present seats, let it be to every one according to his degree.

29. When you meet with one of greater quality than yourself, stop and retire, especially if it be at a door or any straight place, to give way for him to pass.

30. In walking, the highest place in most countries seems to be on the right hand, therefore place yourself on the left of him whom you desire to honor; but if three walk together, the middle place is the most honorable. The wall is usually given to the most worthy if two walk together.

31. If anyone far surpasses others, either in age, estate, or merit, yet would give place to a meaner than himself in his own lodging or elsewhere, the one ought not to except it, so he on the other part should not use much earnestness, nor offer it above once or twice.

32. To one that is your equal, or not much inferior, you are to give the chief place in your lodging, and he to who[m] 'tis offered ought at the first to refuse it, but at the second to accept, though not without acknowledging his own unworthiness.

33. They that are in dignity or in office have in all places precedence, but whilst they are young, they ought to respect those that are their equals in birth or other qualities, though they have no public charge.

34. It is good manners to prefer them to whom we speak before ourselves, especially if they be above us, with whom in no sort we ought to begin.

35. Let your discourse with men of business be short and comprehensive.

36. Artificers and persons of low degree ought not to use many ceremonies to lords or others of high degree but respect and highly honor them, and those of high degree ought to treat them with affability and courtesy, without arrogance.

37. In speaking to men of quality, do not lean nor look them full in the face, nor approach too near them; at least keep a full pace from them.

38. In visiting the sick, do not presently play physician if you be not knowing therein.

39. In writing or speaking, give to every person his due title according to his degree and the custom of the place.

40. Strive not with your superiors in argument, but always submit your judgment to others with modesty.

41. Undertake not to teach your equal in the art [he] himself professes; it flavors of arrogance.

42. Let thy ceremonies in courtesy be proper to the dignity of his place with whom thou converse, for it is absurd to act the same with a clown and a prince.

43. Do not express joy before one sick or in pain, for that contrary passion will aggravate his misery.

44. When a man does all he can though it succeeds not well, blame not him that did it.

45. Being to advise or reprehend anyone, consider whether it ought to be in public or in private, presently or at some other time, in what terms to do it, and in reproving show no sign of choler but do it with all sweetness and mildness.

46. Take all admonitions thankfully in what time or place so ever given, but afterwards, not being culpable, take a time or place convenient to let him know it that gave them.

47. Mock not nor jest at anything of importance, break no jest that are sharp biting, and if you deliver anything witty and pleasant, abstain from laughing thereat yourself.

48. Wherein you reprove another, be unblameable yourself, for example is more prevalent than precepts.

49. Use no reproachful language against anyone, neither curse nor revile.

50. Be not hasty to believe flying reports to the disparagement of any.

51. Wear not your clothes foul, ripped, or dusty, but see they be brushed once every day at least, and take heed that you approach not to any uncleanness.

52. In your apparel be modest and endeavor to accommodate nature, rather than to procure admiration. Keep to the fashion of your equals such as are civil and orderly with respect to times and places.

53. Run not in the streets, neither go too slowly nor with mouth open. Go not shaking your arms, kick not the earth with [your] feet, go not upon the toes nor in a dancing fashion.

54. Play not the peacock, looking everywhere about you to see if you be well decked, if your shoes fit well, if your stockings sit neatly, and clothe[d] handsomely.

55. Eat not in the streets nor in the house out of season.

56. Associate yourself with men of good quality if you esteem your own reputation, for 'tis better to be alone than in bad company.

57. In walking up and down in a house only with one in company, if he be greater than yourself, at the first give him the right hand and stop not till he does, and be not the first that turns, and when you do turn, let it be with your face towards him. If he be a man of great quality, walk not with him cheek by jowl but somewhat behind him, but yet in such a manner that he may easily speak to you.

58. Let your conversation be without malice or envy, for 'tis a sign of a tractable and commendable nature; and in all causes of passion, admit reason to govern.

59. Never express anything unbecoming, nor act against the rules of moral[ity] before your inferiors.

60. Be not immodest in urging your friends to discover a secret.

61. Utter not base and frivolous things amongst grave and learned men, nor very difficult questions or subjects among the ignorant, or things hard to be believed. Stuff not your discourse with sentences amongst your betters nor equals.

62. Speak not of doleful things in a time of mirth or at the table; speak not of melancholy things as death and wounds, and if others mention them, change if you can the discourse. Tell not your dreams but to your intimate friend.

63. A man ought not to value himself of his achievements or rare qualities of wit, much less of his riches, virtue, or kindred.

64. Break not a jest where none take pleasure in mirth; laugh not aloud, nor at all without occasion; deride no man's misfortune, though there seem to be some cause.

65. Speak not injurious words neither in jest nor earnest. Scoff at none although they give occasion.

66. Be not forward but friendly and courteous, the first to salute, hear, and answer, and be not pensive when it's a time to converse.

67. Detract not from others, neither be excessive in commanding.

68. Go not thither where you know not whether you shall be welcome or not. Give not advice without being asked, and when desired, do it briefly.

69. If two contend together, take not the part of either unconstrained, and be not obstinate in your own opinion; in things indifferent, be of the major side.

70. Reprehend not the imperfections of others for that belongs to parents, masters, and superiors.

71. Gaze not on the marks or blemishes of others and ask not how they came. What you may speak in secret to your friend, deliver not before others.

72. Speak not in an unknown tongue in company but in your own language, and that as those of quality do and not as the vulgar. Sublime matters treat seriously.

73. Think before you speak; pronounce not imperfectly nor bring out your words too hastily, but orderly and distinctly.

74. When another speaks, be attentive yourself and disturb not the audience. If any hesitate in his words, help him not nor prompt him without desired, interrupt him not, nor answer him till his speech be ended.

75. In the midst of discourse, ask not of what one treateth, but if you perceive any stop because of your coming, you may well entreat him gently to proceed. If a person of quality comes in while you're conversing, it's handsome to repeat what was said before.

76. While you are talking, point not with your finger at him of whom you discourse, nor approach too near him to whom you talk, especially to his face.

77. Treat with men at fit times about business and whisper not in the company of others.

78. Make no comparisons, and if any of the company be commended for any brave act of virtue, commend not another for the same.

79. Be not apt to relate news if you know not the truth thereof. In discoursing of things you have heard, name not your author. Always a secret discover not.

80. Be not tedious in discourse or in reading, unless you find the company pleased therewith.

81. Be not curious to know the affairs of others, neither approach to those that speak in private.

82. Undertake not what you cannot perform but be careful to keep your promise.

83. When you deliver a matter, do it without passion and with discretion, however mean the person be you do it to.

84. When your superiors talk to anybody, hearken not, neither speak nor laugh.

85. In company of these of higher quality than yourself, speak not till you are asked a question, then stand upright, put off your hat, and answer in few words.

86. In disputes, be not so desirous to overcome as not to give liberty to each one to deliver his opinion, and submit to the judgment of the major part, especially if they are judges of the dispute.

87. Let thy carriage be such as becomes a man grave settled and attentive to that which is spoken. Contradict not at every turn what others say.

88. Be not tedious in discourse, make not many digressions, nor repeat often the same manner of discourse.

89. Speak not evil of the absent, for it is unjust.

90. Being set at meat, scratch not, neither spit, cough, or blow your nose, except [when] there's a necessity for it.

91. Make no show of taking great delight in your victuals, feed not with greediness, cut your bread with a knife, lean not on the table, neither find fault with what you eat.

92. Take no salt or cut bread with your knife greasy.

93. Entertaining anyone at [the] table, it is decent to present him with meat. Undertake not to help others undesired by the master.

94. If you soak bread in the sauce, let it be no more than what you put in your mouth at a time, and blow not your broth at [the] table but stay till [it] cools of itself.

95. Put not your meat to your mouth with your knife in your hand, neither spit forth the stones of any fruit pie upon a dish, nor cast anything under the table.

96. It's unbecoming to stoop much to one's meat. Keep your fingers clean, and when foul, wipe them on a corner of your table napkin.

97. Put not another bit[e] into your mouth till the former be swallowed. Let not your morsels be too big for the jowls.

98. Drink not nor talk with your mouth full; neither gaze about you while you are a drinking.

99. Drink not too leisurely nor yet too hastily. Before and after drinking, wipe your lips; breath[e] not then or ever with too great a noise, for it's uncivil.

100. Cleanse not your teeth with the tablecloth napkin, fork, or knife, but if others do it, let it be done with a pick tooth.

101. Rinse not your mouth in the presence of others.

102. It is out of use to call upon the company often to eat, nor need you drink to others every time you drink.

103. In company of your betters, be not longer in eating than they are; lay not your arm but only your hand upon the table.

104. It belongs to the chiefest in company to unfold his napkin and fall to meat first, but he ought then to begin in time and to dispatch with dexterity that the slowest may have time allowed him.

105. Be not angry at [the] table whatever happens, and if you have reason to be so, show it not but [put] on a cheerful countenance, especially if there be strangers, for good humor makes one dish of meat a feast.

106. Set not yourself at the upper of the table, but if it be your due or that the master of the house will have it so, contend not, lest you should trouble the company.

107. If others talk at [the] table, be attentive but talk not with meat in your mouth.

108. When you speak of God or His attributes, let it be seriously and with reverence. Honor and obey your natural parents although they be poor.

109. Let your recreations be manful, not sinful.

110. Labor to keep alive in your breast that little spark of celestial fire called conscience.

VARIATIONS ON THE GOLDEN RULE

Baha'i Faith
Lay not on any soul a load which you would not wish to be laid upon you, and desire not for anyone the things ye would not desire for yourselves.[78]

—Bahá'u'lláh

Buddhism
Treat not others in ways that you yourself would find hurtful.[79]

—Buddha

Christianity
Therefore all things whatsoever ye would that men should do to you: do ye even so to them: for this is the law and the prophets.[80]

—Jesus

Confucianism
>One word which sums up the basis of all conduct: loving-kindness. Do not impose on others what you do not wish for yourself.[81]

>—Confucius

Hinduism
>This is the sum of duty. Do not unto others that which would cause you pain if done to you.[82]

>—Vyasa

Islam
>As you would have people do to you, do to them; and what you dislike to be done to you, do not do to them.[83]

>—Muhammad

Jainism
>One should treat all creatures in the world as one would like to be treated.[84]

>—Mahavira

Judaism
>That which is despicable to you, do not do to your fellow. This is the whole Torah; and the rest is commentary.[85]

>—Rabbi Hillel

Native Spirituality
>We are as much alive as we keep the earth alive.[86]

>—Chief Dan George

Sikhism
    I am a stranger to no one; and no one is a stranger to me. Indeed, I am a friend to all.[87]

    —**Guru Arjan**

Taoism
    Regard your neighbor's gain as your own gain and your neighbor's loss as your own loss.[88]

    —Lao Tzu

Unitarianism
    Seventh Principle: Respect for the interdependent web of all existence of which we are a part.[89]

Zoroastrianism
Do not do unto others whatever is injurious to yourself.[90]

    —Zoroaster

ABOUT THE AUTHOR

Admittedly, it's unusual for the author not to write his or her own biography. In fact, most authors leap at the chance to present themselves to their readers, usually in ridiculous and highly exaggerated hyperbole, which really serves no purpose, since by the time a reader gets to the author's bio, he or she has already bought the book!

But Shelby Scarbrough is not a "usual" author—or person, for that matter. That's not to say that Shelby is "unusual," but she brings a unique combination of experiences, perspectives, and spirit to her topic, which is what makes this book both important and an interesting read.

I've known Shelby for a longer time than I care to say. We worked together in Ronald Reagan's White House; she was a presidential trip coordinator, and I was a special assistant to the president and assistant press secretary. We traveled the world together, where I watched Shelby gain incredible skills working closely with the highest levels of foreign governments on complicated and sensitive arrangements for visits by the president of the United States.

After leaving the White House staff, Shelby was appointed a

protocol officer in the U.S. State Department, where she served as the government's principal point of contact with heads of state and government visiting the United States.

After leaving the State Department, Shelby went on to a highly successful career as an entrepreneur—including owning ten fast-food restaurants—and as a motivational speaker, not only regaling her audiences in tales of her extraordinary adventures in Washington and around the world, but imparting valuable lessons about how people should treat one another.

That's been her "thing" for as long as I have known her. Even under the most pressured and circumstances, Shelby has always paid special attention to the needs of others. It always bothered her when good manners, mutual respect, and decency were lacking. Whether it was an arrogant colleague at the White House barking orders, a foreign diplomat unreasonably demanding special treatment, or a customer at a restaurant speaking rudely to an employee, Shelby Scarbrough lamented the waning nature of civility—hence this book.

Shelby is a native Californian and a graduate of UCLA and the Harvard Business School's Owner/President Management program, where she was a class graduation speaker. But more importantly, she is a natural optimist who loves the world and believes in the hope of mankind. She is a community builder who genuinely wants to bring people together for the greater good. She's also smart, savvy, and sincere, with no hidden agenda.

She wrote this book not to admonish but to inspire, because she is legitimately concerned about the tone and tenor of how we communicate with each other and the consequences society faces in the absence of civility. Where she has been and what she has seen has convinced her that it all matters. It should be no surprise that her favorite song is an old gospel song sung by Mahalia Jackson called "If

I Can Help Somebody."

In many ways, Shelby's book is a gift to society. Take from it what you will. And above all else, be kind to each other.

—Mark Weinberg, author, columnist, and friend of Shelby

ACKNOWLEDGMENTS

With this rare opportunity, I honor some of the many cherished souls I have encountered along my journey. Thank you for the JOY you all have brought to my life. With love and gratitude to you all.

My Family
The best parents ever, Pattie and Bill Scarbrough
My awesome sisters and their families,
Kelly Scarbrough and Isabella Baccala, Tricia, Greg,
Will and Jack Corcoran

My angels Lindsay Smith Woods, Erin Smith, Keith and Mary Jane Smith, for the years of Joy when I needed it most

Moire Robertson Creek, for letting me call her "best friend" since 7th grade

John T. Walsh (a.k.a "Peter Pan"), for your steadfast friendship, for helping me keep alive the child inside, and for always inspiring me to do good works

Uncle Steve and Aunt Joy Garrison, Aunt Sandi Scarbrough

Cousins Stephanie Garrison Southwick, Mitchell Garrison,
Amy Garrison Olsen, Scott Scarbrough,
Christina and Caroline Hundley
Barbara Safford, Jim and Clayton Harvey,
Laura Rhoades Zungalo and Stephanie Rhoades Hendrix

My Fantastic Teammates
Krista Clive-Smith, Kelley Dold McDonald, Ava Paulazzo, Junna Cayabyab, and THE most incredible editor, Elayne Wells Harmer

To friends and colleagues who, at one point or another, brought joy to my world
Clare Luce Abbey, Andrea and Eric Anderson, Bubu Andres, Thalia Assuras and Michael Johnson, Christy Bakaly, Eric and Chris Bachelor—and their kids Kim, Kendall, and Rob—Shadi Bastani, Amy Bayer, Cheryl and Peter Barnes, Randy Baumgardner, Kirsten Bartok, Terry Baxter, Tony Benedi, Wilma Berends, Mary Ann Best and Dave Millard, Fran Biderman-Gross, Maureen and Mike Birdsall, Joanna Bloor and Randall Reeves, Cindy Boyd, PJ Brady, Barney and Fran Brasseux, Brian Brault, Justin and Sarah Breen, Joe Brennan, Mike and Robin Brennan, Diane Brown, Beth Rustigian Broussalian, Jessica Buchanan, Jennifer Adams Bunker, Gahl Burt, Tract McCone Carr, Meg Carter, Darton and Heather Case, Madeline Connor-Casselberry, Robin Chambers, Meryl and Michael Chertoff, David Chikvaidze, Stuart Chrisp, Kelly Clendenning, Cameron and Korky Creek, Gilberto Crombé, Caroline Cunningham, Maxine Cunningham, Kathy and Scott Dalecio, Brian Daly, Sandi Davis,

ACKNOWLEDGMENTS

Jesus de la Garza, Tom Del Beccaro,
Juliana Del Beccaro De Sa and Sam De Sa, Gabriela Degiorgi,
Becki Donatelli, Frank Donatelli, Joanne and Bill Drake,
Mary Jo Gordon-Dowd and Pat Dowd, JC Duarte,
Elizabeth Dugan, Brooke Dunbar, Jack and Janice Eberly,
Mike and Gina Elliot, Sarah Endline, Marlene Farrell,
Alex Feldman, Cathy Fenton,
Keith Ferrazzi and Kale Yeung,
my teacher Guy Fieri, Lori Fieri, Hunter Fieri and Tara Bernstein,
Larry Fisher, Grier Flinn, Gary Foster, Ann Fragen,
Amb. Lisa Gable,
Bill and Lori Gallagher, George Gan, David,
Lynne and Sarah Galbenski,
Eliot Gattegno, Tom Gibson, Jon Hall, Kelly and Mike Hall,
Jay Handy,
Brian Hansell, Christina Harbridge, David Harmer, Troy Hazard,
Winnie and James Hart, Mary Heitman, Katherine Dudley Hoehn,
Jim Hooley, "Auntie" Sue Hrib, Yvette Irene,
Ben and Mary Jarratt and their children Brigid, Caitlin,
Patrick and Colin,
Mary Jo and Patrick Jephson, Mark David Jones,
Kim Judin, Shannon Jurdana, Sunjay Kapur, Tracy Key, Lena Kline,
Nicole Krakora, Jim Kuhn, Scott and Ann Lane,
Mike and Jim Lake,
Carolyn Layne and Ezio Ciotti, Leslie Lautenslager,
Amb. Frank Lavin,
Jim LeBlanc, Renae Leeza, Mark Lincoln, Rebecca Linder,
Dan Lionello,
Mari Lou Livingood, Tami Cook Lonzo,
Marilyn (Boo), Robert, Wiley and Emily Marsteller,

Cindy White Masley, Tracy Masington and Adam Bendell,
Lew and Leslie, Kelly and Cliff Mathews, Alixe Mattingly,
Penny McAlpin, Anita and Tim McBride, Sharon McBride,
Tim, William, Maggie, Finn, Jack and Angus McDonald,
Brian McKibben,
Nell Merlino, Rich Merryman, Ronit Molko,
Karen Groomes Morgan,
Mick, Nick, Georgie, Dom and Paddy Mullins,
Catherine "Bunny" Murdock, Maroun Nasard, Woodie Neiss,
Tracey "Gnomey" Nicholls, David Nilssen, Kim O'Brien,
Mike and Leila O'Callaghan, Jude Olinger, Monica O'Neill,
Paul O'Neill, Kristen Oliver, Ann, Mitch, Hayden,
Camryn and Chase Ozawa, Joanne Papini, Mary Ann Patterson,
Sherri and Bobby Patton, Bob Peck,
Tom Pernice, Julie and Gregg Petersmeyer,
Amy Weinstein Peterson,
Dr. Cristian and Debbie Pizarro, Darcy Lee Post,
Diane and Ned Powell, Caroline Swanson Price,
Elizabeth and Ken Priestman, Dr. Leo Rastogi,
Anna Rembold, Doug and Lea Robertson and daughters
Tara and Jenna,
Patty Robinson, Selene Rodriguez, Harry Rhoads, Barry Ring,
Avelino Rodriguez, Amb. Selwa "Lucky" Roosevelt, Rodie Rosales,
Michael Ross, Molly Ruland, Marti and Steve Rule,
Warren Rustand,
Annemarie Kerr Ryan, Fred Ryan, Lily Samii, Natasha Sapra and
Bruce Bird, Max and Madeleine Sanasack,
Leah Malone Schaumburg, Bob Schmidt,
Mary Ann and Tim Schultz, Mustapha Shaikh, Andrew Sherman,
Jennifer Sherman, Myles and Terrell Sherman, Victor Shiblie,

Patience Shutts, Margo Simons, Maria, Lyla and Ollie Sipka,
Anne Sittmann, Gerry Sittmann, Eric Slaybaugh, Ashley Parker and
Tim Snider, Pete Souza, Randy Stearns,
Elise Stefanik, Walter Stugger, Grey and Allyson Terry, Peter and
Rita Thomas, Olivia Torres, Rob Trodella, Ken Turteltaub,
Tim Unes, Liza Utter,
Cheryl Visnich, Carole and Bill Waller and her children Caitlin,
Greg and Alyssa,
Ron Walker—and his daughters Lisa, Lynne, and Marja—Kim
Walter,
Jojo Watumull, Erin and Mark "What Are You Wearing" Weinberg,
Keith Williams, Michele Woodward, Bea Wray,
Kim and Gil Wymond,
Andrew and Laura Yeghnazar

**To John Ritter, the Unofficial Mayor of "Noyo,"
and all those he brought together**
Russell and Lori Bay, Donna Bruner, Elia De la Cerda,
Carrie Chanel and Rick Riess, Jim and Susan Clopton,
Dawné Dickenson, Kendall Hoxsey Onysko,
Morgaen Hoxsey Pickett, Anton Denisenko,
Ren and Marilyn Harris,
Rayellen and Mike Jordan and their daughters,
Nina and Bob Klotz, Kathy McClure and Liam,
Scott Owens and Steven Miller, Sheila and Phil Moyer,
Carole Rose, Ally and Sam Selby, Shane and Shannon Wilson,
Brad Tucker, Vivian Ritondale

In Remembrance of Family

Grandparents June and Gene Hundley,
Grandparents Dorothy and Jimmie Mattern
Great-uncle Ed Harvey, Cousin Susan Rhoades,
Uncles Bob and Keith Scarbrough
Uncles Grant and Kent Hundley
Brother-in-law, Gordon Jarratt
Brother-in-law, Bob Baccala

And to friends gone too soon
Rick Ahearn, Ken Behring, Ken Duberstein,
Juanita Duggan, Jodee Desilets and Dr. Bill Norwood,
Anna Ringer, Dave Sanasack, Elizabeth Schreiber,
Bill Sittmann and Paul Spaar

and of course,
Ronald and Nancy Reagan and George Washington

Finally, to Advantage Media | Forbes Books

ENDNOTES

1 A. Ward Burian, *George Washington's Legacy of Leadership* (New York: Morgan James Publishing, 2007).

2 Dandapani's Facebook page, September 5, 2018, https://dandapani.org/blog/where-awareness-goes-energy-flows/.

3 Lawrence C. Becker and Charlotte B. Becker, eds., *Encyclopedia of Ethics* (Abingdon-on-Thames, England: Routledge, 2013), 242.

4 Samuel Johnson, *A Dictionary of the English Language* (London: Longman & Hurst, 1818), s.v. "civility."

5 Ronald Reagan, speech at the Annual Convention of Kiwanis International, July 6, 1987.

6 Jim Rohn, "If You Change Yourself, You Can Change Your Life," *Success* blog, December 13, 2015, https://www.success.com/rohn-if-you-change-yourself-you-can-change-your-life/.

7 Andrew Sherman, interview by the author, October 22, 2019.

8 *Oxford English Dictionary*, 23rd U.S. ed. (New York: Oxford University Press, 1984), s.v. "civility."

9 Ibid., s.v. "courtesy."

10 Ibid., s.v. "manners."

11 Richard Brookhiser, *Founding Father: Rediscovering George Washington* (New York: Free Press, 1996), 130–131.

12 Kevin Butterfield, interview by the author, August 13, 2019.

13 Jonathan Swift, *The Works of the Rev. Jonathan Swift. D.D.*, vol. 10 (London: C. and R. Baldwin, Printers, 1784), 214.

14 Ralph Waldo Emerson, *The Conduct of Life* (Cambridge: Riverside Press, 1860), 187–188.

15 Richard Haass, interview by the author, May 23, 2019.

16 C. S. Lewis, *Mere Christianity* (London: Geoffrey Bies, 1952), 128.

17 Rick Warren, *The Purpose-Driven Life: What on Earth Am I Here For?* (Grand Rapids, MI: Zondervan, 2002), 265.

18 Neel Burton, "Anatomy of Humility," *Outre Monde* (blog), September 3, 2014, https://outre-monde.com/2014/09/03/the-anatomy-of-humility/.

19 Jeff Hyman, "Why Humble Leaders Make the Best Leaders," Forbes.com, October 31, 2018, https://www.forbes.com/sites/jeffhyman/2018/10/31/humility/#705351a41c80.

20 Casey Titus, "One of a Kind? The Humility of George Washington," *History is Now* magazine, February 4, 2018, http://www.historyisnowmagazine.com/blog?tag=George+Washington%27s+humility#.XvPfMC-z1N0.

21 Edward G. Lengel, ed., *A Companion to George Washington* (Hoboken, NJ: Wiley-Blackwell, 2012).

22 Michael L. Stallard and Carolyn Dewing-Hommes, *Fired Up or Burned Out: How to Reignite Your Team's Passion, Creativity, and Productivity* (New York: HarperCollins Leadership, 2009), 119.

23 The phrase is often attributed to President Harry S. Truman, but variants have been used for years. The original aphorism belongs to an English Jesuit priest. A diary entry written by Sir Mountstuart E. Grant Duff on September 21, 1863, noted that Father Strickland said, "I have observed, throughout life, that a man may do an immense deal of good, if he does not care who gets the credit for it."

24 Robert Bennett, interview by the author, October 3, 2019.

25 Audrey Murrell, "Effective Leaders Choose Humility Over Hubris," *Forbes* Magazine website, December 20, 2018, https://www.forbes.com/sites/audreymurrell/2018/12/20/effective-leaders-must-choose-humility-over-hubris/#3a4100a4239d.

26 Recorded by Salmon P. Chase, U.S. Secretary of the Treasury, in his diary, September 22, 1863.

27 Anita McBride, interview by the author, October 1, 2018.

28 Charlie Black, interview by the author, October 4, 2018.

29 Matt. 5:5 (KJV).

30 Matt. 11:29 (KJV).

31 Spencer W. Kimball, speech at Brigham Young University, January 16, 1963.

32 Ibid.

33 Chen Yu-Hsi, "The Buddhist Perception of Humility," International Network on Personal Meaning (website), accessed June 25, 2020, http://www.meaning.ca/archives/archive/art_buddhist-humility_C_Yu_Hsi.htm.

34 Ibid.

35 In Hinduism, a religious and moral law underlying right behavior and social order.

36 Chennai, "Self-control & Humility," *The Hindu* website, updated May 18, 2016, https://www.thehindu.com/features/friday-review/religion/selfcontrol-humility/article5699892.ece.

37 *Oxford English Dictionary*, Vol. 20, 2nd ed. (New York: Oxford University Press, 1989), s.v. "empathy."

38 Frans de Waal, *The Age of Empathy: Nature's Lessons for a Kinder Society* (Portland: Broadway Books, 2010).

39 Andrew Colman, *A Dictionary of Psychology*, 4th ed. (Oxford, England: Oxford University Press, 2015).

40 Abhi Golhar, "10 Ways to Increase Your Emotional Intelligence," Inc.com, September 21, 2018, https://www.inc.com/young-entrepreneur-council/10-ways-to-increase-your-emotional-intelligence.html.

41 "Businessolver Quantifies Empathy in the Workplace," *Businessolver* website, April 12, 2018, https://www.businessolver.com/who-we-are/news/businessolver-quantifies-empathy-in-the-workplace-.

42 "Did You Know?," *Compassion Fatigue Awareness Project* website, accessed July 23, 2020.

43 Malcolm Cowley, "Mister Papa," *LIFE* magazine, January 10, 1949, 90.

44 Cressida Leyshon, "This Week in Fiction: Mohsin Hamid," *The New Yorker*, September 16, 2012.

45 Larry Rulison, "Soldier Who Tracked Down Saddam Says Empathy Broke the Case," (Albany, NY) *Times Union*, April 18, 2018.

46 Ibid.

47 Eric Maddox, "Your Ace of Spades: Using Empathy-based Listening to Build Trust and Find Success," *Speaker Magazine* website, March 2020, http://www.nsaspeaker-magazine.org/nsaspeaker/march_2020/MobilePagedArticle.action?articleId=1566060#articleId1566060.

48 Paul Bloom, *Against Empathy: The Case for Rational Compassion* (New York: Ecco Press, 2016).

49 "[Bloom] prefers a kind of rational compassion—a mixture of caring and detached cost-benefit analysis." Jennifer Senior, "Review: 'Against Empathy,' or the Right Way to Feel Someone's Pain," *The New York Times*, December 6, 2016.

50 Brené Brown, "Boundaries," interview on *The Work of the People: Films for Discovery & Transformation*, March 5, 2016, https://www.theworkofthepeople.com/boundaries.

51 Meryl Chertoff, interview by the author, October 1, 2018.

52 Robert F. Kennedy Jr., "America's Anti-Torture Tradition," *Los Angeles Times*, December 17, 2005.

53 *Norman Rockwell Album*, Norman Rockwell Museum, Stockbridge, Massachusetts.

54 Quote attributed to Rosa Parks.

55 Richard L. Evans, *Richard Evans' Quote Book* (Salt Lake City: Publishers Press, 1971), 244.

56 Nicole Krakora, interview by the author, July 26, 2020.

57 Matthew Lieberman, *Social: Why Our Brains Are Wired to Connect* (New York: Broadway Books, 2014).

58 Ibid.

59 "Alan Alda Wants Us to Have Better Conversations," by Shankar Vedantam, *Hidden Brain* podcast audio, December 17, 2018, https://www.npr.org/2018/12/17/677339713/alan-alda-wants-us-to-have-better-conversations.

60 Fyodor Dostoevsky, *The Brothers Karamazov*, trans. Richard Pevear and Larissa Volokhonsky, 12th ed. (New York: Farrar, Straus and Giroux, 2002), 44.

61 Edmund S. Morgan, *The Genius of George Washington* (New York: W.W. Norton & Company, 1982), 25.

62 Ibid.

63 Thomas Jefferson to Walter Jones, January 2, 1814, *Founders Online*, National Archives, https://founders.archives.gov/documents/Jefferson/03-07-02-0052. [Original source: *The Papers of Thomas Jefferson*, Retirement Series, vol. 7, *28 November 1813 to 30 September 1814*, ed. J. Jefferson Looney (Princeton: Princeton University Press, 2010), 100–104.]

64 Ironically, it's an old Russian proverb. Suzanne Massie, Reagan's adviser on Russian affairs, suggested that he learn a few Russian proverbs in preparation for talks with Mikhail Gorbachev in 1986. The one he liked best was "doveryai no proveryai"—trust, but verify. Barton Swaim, "'Trust, But Verify': An Untrustworthy Political Phrase," *Washington Post*, March 11, 2016.

65 David K. Shipler, "The Summit; Reagan and Gorbachev Sign Missile Treaty and Vow to Work for Greater Reductions," *The New York Times*, December 9, 1987.

66 Gary Thatcher, "Reagan and Gorbachev Play to Mixed Reviews in Moscow," *The Christian Science Monitor*, June 2, 1988.

67 Ibid.

68 Ben Smith, "Transformation, Like Reagan," *POLITICO*, January 16, 2008.

69 Oxford English Dictionary, s.v. "honor."

70 Matt Mullen, "How George Washington's Iron-Willed Single Mom Taught Him Honor," *History Channel* website, last modified February 4, 2020, https://www.history.com/news/george-washington-mother-mary-character-upbringing.

71 Ibid.

72 "Aaron Burr Slays Alexander Hamilton in Duel," *History Channel* website, last modified July 27, 2019, https://www.history.com/this-day-in-history/burr-slays-hamilton-in-duel.

73 Brian Albrecht, "Navy Veteran Robert Shumaker Talks About Surviving as POW During Vietnam," website of *The Plain Dealer* (Cleveland, OH), September 22, 2012, https://www.cleveland.com/metro/2012/09/vietnam_pow_robert_shumaker_sp.html.

74 General Douglas MacArthur, speech to the Corps of Cadets at the U.S. Military Academy at West Point, New York, May 12, 1962.

75 Kent M. Keith, *The Silent Revolution: Dynamic Leadership in the Student Council* (Boston: Harvard Student Agencies, 1968).

76 Oxford English Dictionary, s.v. "honor."

77 Ronald Reagan, inaugural address as governor of California, January 5, 1967.

78 Writings of Bahá'u'lláh, *The Summons of the Lord of Hosts*.

79 Udanavarga 5.18.

80 Matt. 7:12 (KJV).

81 Analects of Confucius 15.23.

82 The Mahabharata 5:1517.

83 Hadith, *Kitab al-Kafi* 2:146.

84 Sutrakritanga 1.11.33.

85 Talmud, *Shabbat* 31a.

86 Wayne Teasdale, *Awakening the Spirit, Inspiring the Soul: 30 Stories of Interspiritual Discovery in the Community of Faiths* (Nashville: SkyLight Paths, 2004).

87 Guru Granth Sahib, 1299.

88 T'ai-Shang Kan-Ying P'ien, 213–218.

89 Ellen Brandenburg, ed., *The Seven Principles in Word and Worship* (Boston: Unitarian Universalist Association, 2007).

90 Shayast-na-Shayast 13.29.

www.ingramcontent.com/pod-product-compliance
Lightning Source LLC
Chambersburg PA
CBHW032049150426
43194CB00006B/461